Oxford Introductions to Language Study

Applied Linguistics

Guy Cook is Professor of Applied
Linguistics at the University of Reading

Published in this series:

Oxford Introductions to Language Study

Series Editor H.G. Widdowson

Applied Linguistics

Guy Cook

OXFORD
UNIVERSITY PRESS

OXFORD
UNIVERSITY PRESS

Great Clarendon Street, Oxford OX2 6DP

Oxford University Press is a department of the University
of Oxford. It furthers the University's objective of excellence
in research, scholarship, and education by publishing
worldwide in

Oxford New York

Auckland Bangkok Buenos Aires Cape Town Chennai
Dar es Salaam Delhi Hong Kong Istanbul Karachi Kolkata
Kuala Lumpur Madrid Melbourne Mexico City Mumbai
Nairobi São Paulo Shanghai Taipei Tokyo Toronto

OXFORD and OXFORD ENGLISH are trade marks of Oxford
University Press in the UK and in certain other countries

First published 2003
Second impression 2003

ISBN 0 19 437598 6

Printed in Hong Kong

Contents

Preface

Purpose

What justification might there be for a series of introductions to language study? After all, linguistics is already well served with introductory texts: expositions and explanations which are comprehensive, authoritative, and excellent in their way. Generally speaking, however, their way is the essentially academic one of providing a detailed initiation into the discipline of linguistics, and they tend to be lengthy and technical: appropriately so, given their purpose. But they can be quite daunting to the novice. There is also a need for a more general and gradual introduction to language: transitional texts which will ease people into an understanding of complex ideas. This series of introductions is designed to serve this need.

Their purpose, therefore, is not to supplant but to support the more academically oriented introductions to linguistics: to prepare the conceptual ground. They are based on the belief that it is an advantage to have a broad map of the terrain sketched out before one considers its more specific features on a smaller scale, a general context in reference to which the detail makes sense. It is sometimes the case that students are introduced to detail without it being made clear what it is a detail *of.* Clearly, a general understanding of ideas is not sufficient: there needs to be closer scrutiny. But equally, close scrutiny can be myopic and meaningless unless it is related to the larger view. Indeed, it can be said that the precondition of more particular enquiry is an awareness of what, in general, the particulars are about. This series is designed to provide this large-scale view of different areas of language study.

As such it can serve as a preliminary to (and precondition for) the more specific and specialized enquiry which students of linguistics are required to undertake.

But the series is not only intended to be helpful to such students. There are many people who take an interest in language without being academically engaged in linguistics *per se*. Such people may recognize the importance of understanding language for their own lines of enquiry, or for their own practical purposes, or quite simply for making them aware of something which figures so centrally in their everyday lives. If linguistics has revealing and relevant things to say about language, this should presumably not be a privileged revelation, but one accessible to people other than linguists. These books have been so designed as to accommodate these broader interests too: they are meant to be introductions to language more generally as well as to linguistics as a discipline.

Design

The books in the series are all cut to the same basic pattern. There are four parts: Survey, Readings, References, and Glossary.

Survey

This is a summary overview of the main features of the area of language study concerned: its scope and principles of enquiry, its basic concerns and key concepts. These are expressed and explained in ways which are intended to make them as accessible as possible to people who have no prior knowledge or expertise in the subject. The Survey is written to be readable and is uncluttered by the customary scholarly references. In this sense, it is simple. But it is not simplistic. Lack of specialist expertise does not imply an inability to understand or evaluate ideas. Ignorance means lack of knowledge, not lack of intelligence. The Survey, therefore, is meant to be challenging. It draws a map of the subject area in such a way as to stimulate thought and to invite a critical participation in the exploration of ideas. This kind of conceptual cartography has its dangers of course: the selection of what is significant, and the manner of its representation, will not be to the liking of everybody, particularly not, perhaps, to some of those inside the discipline. But these surveys are written in the belief that there must be an alternative to a technical account on the one hand and an idiot's guide on the other if linguistics is to be made relevant to people in the wider world.

Readings

Some people will be content to read, and perhaps re-read, the summary Survey. Others will want to pursue the subject and so will use the Survey as the preliminary for more detailed study. The Readings provide the necessary transition. For here the reader is presented with texts extracted from the specialist literature. The purpose of these Readings is quite different from the Survey. It is to get readers to focus on the specifics of what is said, and how it is said, in these source texts. Questions are provided to further this purpose: they are designed to direct attention to points in each text, how they compare across texts, and how they deal with the issues discussed in the Survey. The idea is to give readers an initial familiarity with the more specialist idiom of the linguistics literature, where the issues might not be so readily accessible, and to encourage them into close critical reading.

References

One way of moving into more detailed study is through the Readings. Another is through the annotated References in the third section of each book. Here there is a selection of works (books and articles) for further reading. Accompanying comments indicate how these deal in more detail with the issues discussed in the different chapters of the Survey.

Glossary

Certain terms in the Survey appear in bold. These are terms used in a special or technical sense in the discipline. Their meanings are made clear in the discussion, but they are also explained in the Glossary at the end of each book. The Glossary is cross-referenced to the Survey, and therefore serves at the same time as an index. This enables readers to locate the term and what it signifies in the more general discussion, thereby, in effect, using the Survey as a summary work of reference.

Use

The series has been designed so as to be flexible in use. Each title is separate and self-contained, with only the basic format in common. The four sections of the format, as described here, can be drawn upon and combined in different ways, as required by the needs, or interests, of different readers. Some may be content with the Survey and the Glossary and may not want to follow up the suggested References. Some may not wish to venture into the Readings. Again, the Survey might be considered as appropriate preliminary reading for a course in applied linguistics or teacher education, and the Readings more appropriate for seminar discussion during the course. In short, the notion of an introduction will mean different things to different people, but in all cases the concern is to provide access to specialist knowledge and stimulate an awareness of its significance. This series as a whole has been designed to provide this access and promote this awareness in respect to different areas of language study.

H.G. WIDDOWSON

Author's Acknowledgements

Though short, this book has been through many drafts. It proved, to my surprise, far more exacting to write than a longer book—and in the middle I nearly gave up. There are a number of people whose help and friendship has kept me going. Thanks are due to Cristina Whitecross at OUP for her efficiency and encouragement, Kieran O'Halloran, Alison Sealey, and Tony Smith for enlightening discussion and advice, Elena Poptsova Cook for support and inspiration. I also thank Anne Conybeare for improving the manuscript in its final stages. But most of all, my greatest thanks go to the series editor, Henry Widdowson, for pursuing every point in every draft so critically but so constructively.

GUY COOK

Survey

1

Applied linguistics

The need for applied linguistics

Language is at the heart of human life. Without it, many of our most important activities are inconceivable. Try to imagine relating to your family, making friends, learning, falling in love, forming a relationship, being a parent, holding—or rejecting—a religious faith, having political ideals, or taking political action, without using words. There are other important activities, of course, which do seem to exist without language. Sexual relations, preparing and eating food, manual labour and crafts, the visual arts, playing and listening to music, wondering at the natural world, or grieving at its destruction. Yet even these are often developed or enhanced through language. We would perceive them quite differently had we never read about them or discussed them.

Throughout history and across the world, people have used language to gossip and chat, flirt and seduce, play games, sing songs, tell stories, teach children, worship gods, insult enemies, pass on information, make deals, remember the past, and lament the dead. Such activities seem to be intrinsic to human life, as natural to us as flight is to birds. People do them without conscious analysis. It does not seem that we need to know about language to use it effectively.

Language use, then, is in many ways a natural phenomenon beyond conscious control. Yet there are also aspects of language use in which we can intervene and about which, consequently, there are decisions to be made. In making these decisions there are many questions and subsidiary questions to be asked, each one admitting many different and opposed answers. Take, for example, language in education.

- What language skills should children attain beyond basic literacy? (And what is basic literacy anyway? Reading and writing, or something more?)
- Should children speaking a dialect be encouraged to maintain it or steered towards the **standard** form of a language? (And, if so, how is that standard form decided and by whom?)
- In communities with more than one language which ones should be used in schools? (And does every child have a right to be educated in the language they use at home?)
- Should deaf children learn a sign language, or a combination of lip reading and speaking? (And are sign languages as complex as spoken ones?)
- Should everyone learn foreign languages and, if so, which one or ones? (And what is the best way to learn and teach them?)
- Should every child study literature? (And, if so, should it be established works or more modern ones? And should they study just their own national literature or that of other countries?)

Such language issues, however, are by no means confined to the school. On the contrary, these educational dilemmas echo those of society at large.

- Languages change. Should this just be accepted as an inevitable fact or should change be controlled in some way?
- Some languages are dying out. Should that be prevented and, if so, how?
- Should the growth of English as the international **lingua franca** be welcomed or deplored?
- Is it better for people to learn each other's languages or use translations? (And what is accurate or 'good' translation? Could it ever be done by computer?)
- Is language being used for political oppression and indoctrination? (And, if so, should something be done about it?)
- Which languages should be used in law courts and official documents?

All of these questions, and many more like them, demand

answers. In the contemporary world, with its rapid and radical changes, many of them take on a new significance and seem more pressing than they have in the past. To answer them it seems reasonable that we should set out to investigate and understand the facts of language use, to organize and formalize what we know, and to subject our knowledge to rational consideration and critical analysis. Only by doing so will we be able to set out the options for action and the reasoning behind them, and to debate the alternatives openly and independently, in as informed and rational a manner as possible. This is the aim—and the aspiration—of **applied linguistics**, the academic discipline concerned with the relation of knowledge about language to decision making in the real world.

Examples and procedures

On the basis of this definition, then, we can say that applied linguistics sets out to investigate problems in the world in which language is implicated—both educational and social problems like those listed above. Our provisional definition is, of course, very abstract and general, so we might give it some substance by considering a few concrete examples. In what kind of problems is language implicated? How might they be investigated?

Here are a number of imaginary but representative situations in which decisions about language need to be taken.

- The head teacher of a London school is thinking of offering another foreign language in addition to French. The options are Chinese (the world's largest first language), Spanish (one of the world's largest and most widely distributed languages), or the Indian language Gujarati (the largest second language in the school and local community, and one which has approximately forty-three million speakers worldwide). Which of these languages should be taught, and why?
- A business executive wants to learn Japanese in preparation for taking up a post in Tokyo. There are three courses available. Course One has a strong emphasis on learning to write. Course Two focuses on the spoken language, claiming that learning to write too early is demotivating. It does, however, explain the rules of Japanese grammar in English and

use translation. Course Three's approach is 'natural', with no translation or explanation of rules, but only a series of communicative classroom activities and tasks. Which course is the best choice, and why?

– A business in the USA exports industrial machinery to South America. There are frequently financial, legal, and safety documents to translate, and it is important that these are accurate. The firm employs two translators: Juan, a sixty-year-old Cuban émigré who once ran a similar business, and twenty-two-year-old Jemima, who studied Spanish literature at a prestigious university. Juan complains to the management that Jemima's translation of some safety regulations is full of errors. Jemima says this is nonsense, and there is a terrible row. None of the managers speak Spanish themselves. How can they judge between them?

– Zramzshra is a small (fictional) island in the Indian Ocean. The Zramzshraran language uses a unique alphabet which developed from the Phoenician alphabet when traders came to the island 3,000 years ago. Zramzshra's Finance Minister argues for a reform in which this alphabet will be replaced by the Roman alphabet (the one used in English and many other languages). This change, he argues, will make the island's life easier and more prosperous, with benefits for English teaching, computer-mediated communication, trade, and tourism. Is this the best policy?

In responding to such language related problems, we can draw upon common sense and experience to judge what action should be taken. But in recommending a particular course of action we might benefit both from more information and from a more systematic approach. For example, we might study what other people have said on similar matters, and we might make investigations of our own, perhaps by interviewing the parents and children in the school, observing some Japanese lessons, consulting a third Spanish speaker, and so on. And when—as sadly often happens—the advice we offer, well-informed though it might be, is ignored for political or commercial reasons, or out of prejudice, we might wish to form a pressure group to put across our case more effectively. It is these processes of study, reflection, investigation, and action which constitute applied linguistics as an academic discipline.

The scope of applied linguistics

Since language is implicated in so much of our daily lives, there is clearly a large and open-ended number of quite disparate activities to which applied linguistics is relevant. So even with these examples, the scope of applied linguistics remains rather vague. To get at a more precise definition of the field we need to be more specific. We need not just to give examples but to classify the kinds of problem we are concerned with in a systematic way, and so map out the scope of our area. In other words, we need to refer specific instances to more general conceptual areas of study. These areas can be identified under three headings as follows:

1 *Language and education*
   This area includes:

   first-language education, when a child studies their home language or languages.

   additional-language education, often divided into **second-language education**, when someone studies their society's majority or official language which is not their home language, and **foreign-language education**, when someone studies the language of another country.

   clinical linguistics: the study and treatment of speech and communication impairments, whether hereditary, developmental, or acquired (through injury, stroke, illness, or age).

   language testing: the assessment and evaluation of language achievement and proficiency, both in first and additional languages, and for both general and specific purposes.

2 *Language, work, and law*
   This area includes:

   workplace communication: the study of how language is used in the workplace, and how it contributes to the nature and power relations of different types of work.

   language planning: the making of decisions, often supported by legislation, about the official status of languages and their institutional use, including their use in education.

   forensic linguistics: the deployment of linguistic evidence in criminal and other legal investigations, for example, to establish the authorship of a document, or a profile of a speaker from a tape-recording.

3 *Language, information, and effect*
This area includes:

literary stylistics: the study of the relationship between linguistic choices and effects in literature.

Critical Discourse Analysis (CDA): the study of the relationship between linguistic choices and effects in persuasive uses of language, of how these indoctrinate or manipulate (for example, in marketing and politics), and the counteracting of this through analysis.

translation and interpretation: the formulation of principles underlying the perceived equivalence between a stretch of language and its translation, and the practices of translating written text and interpreting spoken language.

information design: the arrangement and presentation of written language, including issues relating to **typography** and layout, choices of medium, and effective combinations of language with other means of communication such as pictures and diagrams.

lexicography: the planning and compiling of both monolingual and bilingual dictionaries, and other language reference works such as thesauri.

All of these areas fall within our definition of applied linguistics and are claimed as areas of enquiry by organizations and journals concerned with the discipline. Yet in practice some of them are more independent than others. Clinical linguistics and translation studies in particular are often regarded as independent disciplines. Among the others some—such as the study of foreign language learning—are more active as areas of academic enquiry than others.

It will not be possible in this short book to cover all of these areas in detail. Inevitably, examples will be selective, and many important matters will be omitted. The aim is rather to seek out key themes and to set out the ideas and procedures that underlie and unite their study.

Linguistics and applied linguistics: a difficult relationship

One way of approaching the practical and professional problems of these areas is by relating them to what has been said about language in **linguistics**—the academic discipline concerned with the study of language in general. Like any discipline, linguistics looks for generalities underlying actual appearances, and so in some degree is bound to represent an abstract idealization of language rather than the way it is experienced in the real world. How closely the resulting models of language correspond with experience will vary considerably, and there are different and opposed schools of linguistics to draw upon.

One particularly influential type of idealization is that used in the **generative linguistics** introduced by Noam Chomsky from the late 1950s onward. In his view, the proper subject matter of linguistics should be the representation of language in the mind (**competence**), rather than the way in which people actually use language in everyday life (**performance**). Chomsky's claim is that this internal language is essentially biological rather than social and is separate from, and relatively uninfluenced by, outside experience. It is to be investigated not through the study of actual language use in context but rather through the consideration of invented sentences intuitively felt to be acceptable instances of the language. The relationship between this highly abstract model and ordinary experience of language is very remote. The question for applied linguistics is whether such a connection can be made and, if so, what can then be made of the connection.

Chomsky's linguistics, however, is not the only kind. In **sociolinguistics**, the focus is—as the name suggests—very much upon the relation between language and society. Sociolinguistics endeavours to find systematic relationships between social groupings and contexts, and the variable ways in which languages are used. In **functional linguistics** the concern is with language as a means of communication, the purposes it fulfils, and how people actually use their language. In recent years a particularly important development in the investigation of language use has been **corpus linguistics**. In this approach, vast databanks containing millions of words of actual language in use can be searched within seconds to yield extensive information about word frequencies and combinations which is not revealed by intuition.

These approaches to linguistic study seem much closer to the reality of experience than Chomsky's, and therefore more relevant to the concerns of applied linguistics. Yet they, too, in their different ways and for their different purposes, abstract and idealize, detaching language from the experience of its use. Their purpose moreover is to describe and explain and not, as in applied linguistics, to engage with decision making. What is needed in all cases—and perhaps particularly in those approaches where the relevance of linguistics seems self-evident—is constant **mediation** between two discourses or orders of reality: that of everyday life and language experience, and that represented by abstract analyses of linguistic expertise. The two are very different and difficult to reconcile, but the attempt to make each relevant to the other is the main challenge for applied linguistics and the justification for its existence.

Linguistic theory and description cannot, then, be deployed directly to solve the problems with which applied linguistics is concerned. One important reason is the nature of the problems themselves. They, too, like models of linguistics, represent certain perspectives on reality. Applied linguistics is not simply a matter of matching up findings about language with pre-existing problems but of using findings to explore how the perception of problems might be changed. It may be that when problems are reformulated from a different point of view they become more amenable to solution. This changed perception may then, in turn, have implications for linguistics.

The methodology of applied linguistics must therefore be complex. It must refer to the findings and theories of linguistics, choosing among the different schools and approaches, and making these theories relevant to the problem in hand. At the same time, it must investigate and take into account the experience and needs of the people involved in the problem itself. It must then seek to relate these two perspectives to each other, attempting perhaps, in the process, to reformulate each. And it must undertake investigation and theorizing of its own.

Conceived of in this way, applied linguistics is a quest for common ground. It establishes a reciprocal relationship between experience and expertise, between professional concerns with language problems and linguistics. In the chapters that follow we shall explore these relationships further as they unfold in specific areas and issues.

2
Prescribing and describing: popular and academic views of 'correctness'

At the heart of the aspiration to relate theory to practice is a constant tension between language as viewed by 'the expert' and language as everyone's lived experience—including the applied linguist's own. The two are by no means easily reconciled and, as in other areas of academic enquiry affecting everyday life, are likely to be aggravated by any attempt to impose insensitively an 'expert' view which runs contrary to deeply held belief. Nowhere is this more apparent than in our attitudes to the language education of children, and the beliefs which they reflect about the 'best' language use. These provide a good illustration of the kind of problematic issues with which applied linguistic enquiry engages.

Children's language at home and school

As every parent knows, young children speak idiosyncratically. A child growing up in an English-speaking family, for example, might say 'I brang it', even though everyone around them says 'I brought it' to mean the same thing. Even when the child does say 'I brought it', they may still not pronounce the words as adults do. They might, for example, say 'I bwort it'. Parents—even the most anxious ones—are usually indulgent of such deviations. They are the stuff of anecdotes and affectionate memories rather than serious concern. It is clear, after all, what the child is saying, and most idiosyncrasies disappear of their own accord.

At school, however, the situation is very different. Here the child is expected, and taught, to use language 'correctly'. Not only are English-speaking children expected to say the words 'I brought it' clearly and properly pronounced, but also to write them correctly spelt (or should that be spelled?) and punctuated. So not only is 'I brang it' wrong, but also, in writing, are 'I brort it', and 'I brought, it'. Indeed, teaching children their own national language is, in many people's view, synonymous with eliminating such deviations. A good deal of school time is spent on this task, and a good deal of the child's educational success will depend upon the results.

In the case of pre-school 'brang' or 'bwort' there is little to be concerned about. In school, however, the issue of what counts as correct is much more complex. What of the child who, through some speech impediment, never does make the transition from 'bwort' to 'brought'? What of the child who pronounces 'I brought it' in a regional accent with an *ah* sound as 'I brart it', or says 'I seen it' (instead of 'I saw it'), not for some short-lived developmental reason, but because this is what their family and friends say too, as part of their dialect? What of the child who has recently moved to Britain from the USA and says, as their parents do, 'I've gotten it' instead of 'I've got it', and writes 'color' instead of 'colour'? Should the teacher eliminate these dialectal and national variations, thus seeming to correct the parents as well? The voices of school and home are not always the same. To make matters more complex still, a third voice—the voice of the peer group—speaks ever louder and more persuasively as children grow older. They put 'RU' instead of 'are you' in text messages; they give words different fashionable senses, invent new ones, and include slang or swear words of which the adults disapprove, even if they use them themselves.

Within the school context by far the most controversial aspect of this situation involves the relationship of the **standard** form of the language to **dialects**. The standard is generally used in written communication, taught in schools, and codified in dictionaries and grammar books. Dialects are regional and social-class varieties of the language which differ from the standard in pronunciation, grammar, and vocabulary, and are seldom written down at all. The teaching of the standard can be viewed in two quite contradictory ways. On the one hand it can be seen as conferring an unfair advantage upon those children who already speak a variety close to it, while simultaneously denying the worth of other dialects and damaging the heritage of those children who speak them. On the other hand, given that the standard exists, has prestige and power, and provides a gateway to written knowledge, it can be argued that teaching it helps to give an equal opportunity to all. In support of this latter view, there is no reason why children cannot grow up knowing both a dialect and the standard form, valuing both in different ways and using them appropriately according to context.

In educational theory, from the 1960s onwards, this ongoing debate has been further aggravated and complicated by the claim, made by the educational sociologist Basil Bernstein, that some social-class variations indicate not only differences but **deficits**. In Bernstein's view, the language used in some sections of society is a **restricted code** which lacks the full resources of the more **elaborated code** of the standard. Not surprisingly, this view has been hotly contested by others who argue that all varieties are equally complex, functional, and expressive.

Schools are a good barometer of both language use and social values, and their approach to teaching the national language or languages, which is much the same all over the world, arises from two interesting facts. The first fact is that a language—any language—is subject to enormous variation. There are differences between individuals, social groups, generations, and nations, and language is used differently in speech and writing, and in formal and informal situations. The second fact is that many people are intolerant of this variation. They struggle for a single 'standard' way of using the language and care very deeply about achieving this norm. This is why there is general support for schools in their attempt to teach a standard form of the language to all pupils, and why many people get so hot under the collar about anything they perceive as incorrect, whether it be the 'dropping' of *h* at the beginning of words, failure to distinguish 'who' from 'whom', or the use of new words such as 'flammable' for 'inflammable'. Objections to such language can be very strong, and low personal morals are often imputed to its perpetrators. 'Incorrect' language is seldom seen as just different, but is typically described as 'wrong', 'lazy', 'slovenly', 'degenerate', 'dirty', 'illogical', or 'corrupt'. Yet while there is general agreement over the need for a standard and the need to preserve standards—the two words are, of course, related—there is often disagreement over the details, and when this happens there can be some very bitter arguments indeed. For example, should 'all right' be written as two words, as it used to be taught, or as a single word 'alright', as it is often taught now?

Given the depth of feeling which such apparently trivial differences can arouse, applied linguistics needs to approach such debates with both caution and respect. If it is to engage with the people who are in the thick of decision making about which forms are acceptable in which contexts, then a major task is not only to understand the nature of variation in the system itself, but also why this variation can be such an emotive issue.

Description versus prescription

Where in such cases of disagreement over usage can people appeal for authority? One obvious answer might be to linguistics, the academic discipline charged with the study of language. There, surely, decisive and authoritative judgements can be found? However, the response of academic linguists to this general public concern for correctness has only added fuel to the fire, uniting the advocates of both 'all right' and 'alright' in a common cause! For they have generally argued, not for one side or the other, but that all variants are equally valid simply by virtue of the fact that they occur, and that no one form is any more or less correct than another. As in the natural sciences, they argue, the task is not to evaluate but to describe and explain. A botanist, for example, should describe and explain the facts about plants, not tell you which plants are the most beautiful. Thus linguists tend to favour **description** (saying what does happen) over **prescription** (saying what ought to happen) and argue that, from a linguistics point of view, the standard is neither superior nor more stable than any other variety. To justify their views they point to such facts as the following:

1 If there was never any deviation from the norm then languages would never change. We would all still be saying 'Wherefore art thou?' instead of 'Why are you?'

2 If a single standard was absolute and unassailable then regional standards would never gain independence. Webster's *American Dictionary of the English Language* would have the same

standing as a bad piece of school work, and it would be as incorrect to write 'color' in Washington as in London.

3 Dialects have their own consistent rule governed grammars, every bit as complex and expressive as those of standard forms. The so-called double negative—'I didn't do nothing', for example, often castigated as sloppy and illogical—is used with consistency in certain dialects of English, and equivalents can be found in the standard forms of other languages such as Italian '*Non ho fatto niente*' and Russian '*Nichego ne sdelal*'.

4 The standard form of a language is often very similar to the usage of the most economically and politically powerful class or region, for example southern England in Britain and Castile in Spain. It can be regarded as a dominant dialect which, for political rather than linguistic reasons, has been elevated and codified. Consequently, when the balance of power changes, so does the notion of the standard. The emergence of American English as an alternative standard to British English is a textbook example.

5 The grammar of written language differs considerably from that of speech, even among speakers whose variety is closest to the standard, and writing carries more prestige and authority. As the standard is often the only form of the language used in writing, what often happens in debates about correctness is that written forms, for example, 'Whom do you want?', are imposed rather self-consciously on speech.

6 Some supposedly correct forms have been invented and imposed by grammarians through analogy with another language. Probably the best-known example in English is the claim, based on a rule imported from Latin, that one should say 'This is I' instead of 'This is me'.

While all of these arguments appear to have a kind of relentless logic to them, they depend on a detachment from social reality and are very much at odds with a deeply felt public view of language. It is all very well to say that, linguistically speaking, correctness is not a valid concept, but to many people deciding what counts as correct is *the* single most important issue about their language, and for linguistics, the discipline which claims to study language, to refuse to engage with this debate is perceived as at best incomprehensible, and at worst subversive and perverse. Linguists may assume a superior air and insist that their concern is with objective description, but in taking this stance they necessarily distance themselves from people's everyday experience of language.

For these reasons, on occasions when they have argued their case in public, linguists have usually aroused irate opposition, and then—feeling bruised but superior—they have hastily retreated back into their academic sanctuaries. This isolationism, though sad, might have some justification. Linguists' concern is knowledge as an end in itself rather than with action based upon that knowledge. For applied linguistics, however, withdrawal is not an option; it is committed by definition to engagement with 'problems in the world in which language is implicated'. It cannot turn its back upon such matters as the policy for teaching a national language in schools. Applied linguists have a responsibility to investigate the reasons behind the impasse between descriptivists and prescriptivists (itself a problem involving language), to engage with the practical consequences of holding one view or another, and to mediate between academic and public concerns. They must relate to, and negotiate between, the descriptivist view, often used to support the claim that the standard form is merely a political convenience perpetuating the privilege of a minority, and the prescriptivist view—ironically often held by speakers whose dialect differs most sharply from it—that there is something intrinsically 'superior' and 'better' about the standard.

We might observe that, as is so often the case in such disputes, it is certainly not that academic experts are necessarily right and lay opinion just wrong-headed. Academics do not have a monopoly either on knowledge or on rational argument. The same is true in many analogous domains—for example, medicine, nutrition, or childcare—where everyday activity, vital to people's well-being, is also the subject of academic research. Thus, while there is force in descriptivist arguments, there are also valid reservations to be made about them:

1 To talk about a language at all, there must be some pre-existing notion of what does and does not count as an example. Descriptivists may accept, as instances, some examples of dialectal forms which hard-line prescriptivists would exclude, but there are always others—from another

language for example—which they reject. Thus, they are drawing the boundary around a language in a different place, not abandoning the notion of boundaries altogether.

2 In deciding what does count as an example of the language, linguists often base their decisions upon native-speaker use or judgement. This, however, simply shifts the criterion away from what is said to the person who says it. It also runs the danger of becoming circular, i.e. native speakers provide valid examples of the language; valid examples of the language are provided by native speakers.

3 Despite descriptivist insistence on the equality of all varieties, it is nevertheless the standard which is most often used in their analyses while other varieties are described as departures from it.

4 If linguists are concerned with describing and explaining facts about language, then the widespread belief in prescriptivism, and the effect of this belief on language use, is itself a fact about language which needs describing and explaining.

5 Paradoxically, to advocate description and outlaw prescription is itself prescriptive.

An applied linguistics perspective

There is clearly material here for a head-on collision—and this indeed is what regularly happens when the two sides exchange views. The arguments on both sides, however, are not easily influenced either by appeals to logic or to evidence. This is because adherence to one side or the other is often as much emotional and ideological as rational. Descriptivists, on the one hand, are passionate believers in an objective science of language; prescriptivists, on the other, feeling that their very identity and heritage is at stake, have an equally strong desire to impose conformity. Given the incompatibility of the two views, it is unrealistic that people holding either will simply make way for the other. To make any headway, applied linguistics has the very difficult task of trying to find points of contact in the contrary views so that necessary decisions can be made.

Perhaps the first step is to recognize that, as points of view, they can be taken as different perceptions which need not be seen as competing alternatives. Thus it is unquestionably the case, as descriptivists tell us, that all language varies, that all language carries markers of social identity, and that there is no way of establishing the relative superiority of a form of speaking on linguistic grounds, so that when varieties are preferred or stigmatized it can only be for sociopolitical or ideological reasons. One cannot legitimately use description for prescriptive purposes; one cannot, for example, promote the cause of standard English by appealing to the superior logic inherent in its grammar. Conversely, it is a social fact that different forms of speaking are indeed privileged or stigmatized, that people find security in stability and resist change, and that proper or correct behaviour, whether linguistic or not, is inextricably involved with a sense of cultural identity. In short, prescription is a social phenomenon and it cannot legitimately be countered by description.

Whatever the merits of the rival arguments for descriptivism and prescriptivism—and there is certainly a degree of truth on both sides—in many practical activities it is simply impossible to proceed without some notion of correct language use. In the cases of speech therapy, foreign language teaching, and language testing, for example, it is hard to see how the activity could exist at all if there were not some yardstick to measure success. Criteria of correctness may change—and they are more often implicit than explicit—but they must nevertheless exist. A major task for applied linguistics is to bring out what these criteria are and how they are decided. If it is to inform practical decision making, applied linguistics must first investigate what it means to know a language and to use it well, presenting its findings in ways which are relevant and useful to professionals such as teachers and speech therapists, who necessarily have to act as though they knew the answers to these impossible questions.

This is not to say that it is possible to present answers which are absolute and stable. On the contrary, applied linguistics is denied the luxury of those easier solutions which are available to both academics disengaged from the urgencies of practice, and to non-academics confident that they have nothing to learn from research. Ideas about language are constantly shifting, both in the light of new theories and findings, and under the impact of non-linguistic factors such as demographic and political change. Findings are inherently provisional, flexible, and open to constant challenge. Consequently, applied linguistics must engage with messy and disputable areas. Without undermining the rationale for its own existence, it cannot avoid controversy.

In Britain, for example, the educational dilemma about standard and dialect forms has been a highly charged and emotive issue, concerning as it does the rights and futures of children, and issues of social advantage and disadvantage. It is also a classic applied linguistic problem. From the 1980s, applied linguists were involved in a series of government committees making recommendations on the teaching of English in schools. Yet, as so often the case in such debates, opinions became polarized and simplified, and more thoughtful recommendations tended to be sidelined or ignored by politicians. (This course of events is again in itself an applied linguistic problem.) Clearly it is not enough, in such policy-making arenas, for the applied linguist only to give learned and informed advice. He or she also needs to have strategies for engaging with and exerting influence upon the realities of decision making. If people do—at least in modern literate societies—have a strong disposition towards establishing norms of correctness, if they do have to act upon their beliefs even when the reasons for them are not entirely clear, then it is essential to negotiate with those attitudes and beliefs, to build them into our model, to participate as well as to observe.

There is, however, something in this necessary troubleshooting which gives applied linguistics an edge, both over other branches of linguistics and over decision making not informed by theory and research. Precisely because it must consider both perspectives, it can contribute a richer understanding than either. Language is a lived experience intimately involved with people's sense of worth and identity. It does not lend itself to easy or simple answers, and it cannot for this reason be treated, even when studied as an academic discipline, in the same cold and impersonal way as astronomy or mechanics, for if we do treat it in this way we lose something of its essential nature. Yet language also has aspects of a nature that eludes casual speculation, and that can be enriched by institutionalized reflection and academic research. The task of applied linguistics is to mediate between these two very different perspectives. This is a difficult task, but it is what applied linguistics does and what makes it worthwhile.

3
Languages in the contemporary world

In Chapter 2, we focused attention on the difference between the way linguists describe a language and the way it is experienced by its speakers in everyday life. People also have experience of, and ideas about, languages other than their own, and this will be the concern of the present chapter.

Language and languages

In Chapter 1, we provisionally defined applied linguistics as investigating 'problems in the world in which language is implicated'. The term 'language' is used in the singular, as though language were a single unitary phenomenon. Yet, although languages have common properties, from the point of view of their users it is the differences that count. People do not speak 'language' as an abstraction, but particular languages. And from a practical perspective the most salient feature is that these languages are mutually incomprehensible. When we hear an unknown language, we cannot even make out the boundaries between words. Reading it is no better because, even if it uses familiar symbols, we do not know what the words mean. And even if we painstakingly tracked down each word in a dictionary, we would still not understand the way they combine, or change in form and meaning with different contexts.

These simple facts mean that one of the main 'problems in which language is implicated' is how speakers of different languages can communicate with each other. There are two possible solutions: one is for one, or both, sets of speakers to learn the other's language, and the other is to employ a translator.

In Chapter 4 we shall be concerned with language teaching and learning, and in Chapter 6 with translation. But before we address these matters directly, we need to consider how differences between languages are perceived not only by linguists but by non-specialists too. We need also to examine the balance of languages in the contemporary world and the factors which determine who learns whose language, and why.

Attitudes to languages

Native speakers of a language usually regard it as in some sense their own property. Yet they do not resent other people acquiring it: they lose nothing in the process and are flattered to share something so highly valued. Yet, however many people learn their language, they still regard it as 'theirs'. They feel that outsiders cannot identify with it quite as they do. To them it remains familiar and intrinsic, to others it remains foreign and something apart. It is their right, they believe—as we have seen in Chapter 2—to determine what counts as correct and acceptable.

These strong views extend beyond the forms of the language to people's general characterizations of their own language—and of other people's languages too. Here again, as with the issue of correctness, there is a marked difference between popular and academic beliefs. Thus, while linguists regard all languages as equal and arbitrary systems capable of fulfilling the same functions, this is far from how they are perceived by language users. Some languages are popularly regarded as being less complex than others. For example, one reason often given for the spread of international English is that it is easier to learn. Some languages are regarded as being more beautiful, and all are regarded as carrying the 'spirit' of a particular nation or people. Thus Latin is widely believed to be more logical, or German more efficient, or French more romantic than other languages, and so on. These are all views which we must take into account if we are to mediate between the academic and the popular perspective.

Language users have their own views, too, about what counts as a separate language and what does not. Here it is the linguists who are in a difficult position. For although linguistics investigates languages either in terms of their history or in terms of their formal similarities, it is neither of these perspectives which determines the boundaries between them. Nor is the boundary between languages, as popularly believed, a matter of mutual comprehensibility. There are many cases where people who are said to speak the same language cannot understand each other. The dialect of Sicily makes little sense in Venice, for example, and vice versa, though both are described as 'Italian'. Cantonese and Putonghua (Mandarin Chinese)—mutually incomprehensible when spoken—are both referred to as 'Chinese'. On the other hand, there are pairs of languages which are, in part anyway, mutually comprehensible but are regarded as different. Speakers of Russian can guess at the meaning of Ukrainian; Italian may work for basic transactions in a Spanish-speaking country; readers of Japanese can make some headway with Chinese characters ('borrowed' by the Japanese writing system over a thousand years ago).

The awkward fact is that if people decree that they speak a distinct language, or conversely that what they speak is a dialect of a larger language, then it is difficult to argue with them. Linguists, despite their claims to dispassionate objectivity and detachment, by accepting terms such as 'Italian', 'Chinese', or 'English', are working with categories which are not based on any very clear or scientific criteria at all.

The languages of nations: boundaries and relationships

In addition to academic linguistic and popular approaches, there are two other ways in which languages can be compared, both of which are of particular importance in the contemporary world. These are by numbers of speakers and by geographical distribution. While the world's largest languages, such as Chinese, English, Hindi, Spanish, and Arabic, have hundreds of millions of speakers and are frequently used beyond their homelands, the majority of the world's languages are much smaller, some with only a few hundred speakers. Smaller languages are confined to restricted areas and specific ethnic groups, and are often vulnerable. Among the world's estimated 6,000 languages, **language death** now occurs increasingly frequently. It has been estimated that half of the world's languages are likely to disappear in the twenty-first century.

The constantly changing nature of languages suggests that their fates, and the boundaries between them, reflect not so much either formal linguistic descriptions or popular ideas, as historical and political forces. Powerful nations have frequently asserted their unity by promoting one single majority language in a standard written form while simultaneously suppressing or ignoring minority languages. Yet there is also an ironic consequence to the successful promotion of one language. In those nations which have spread their language beyond their own borders the result has often been a multiplication rather than a reduction of the languages within them. In the aftermath of empire, the capitals of the larger European nations—the most adamant exponents of *mono*lingualism—have become some of the most *multi*lingual places on earth. A survey of London primary schools in 2000 revealed that a total of 350 home languages are used by London schoolchildren. The situations of Paris, Rome, and Berlin are not dissimilar. Also, independence movements within officially monolingual nations often associate their cause with the promotion of one of the indigenous languages which the state has pushed aside. Scots Gaelic, to give but one example, once brutally repressed, has been championed by the Scottish National Party and is now an official language of the Scottish Parliament—even though few members can actually speak it!

Despite the efforts of nation builders then, the monolingual state remains a myth. All nations have substantial linguistic groups within their borders, making cross-linguistic communication an *intra*national as well as an *inter*national affair. On a personal level this means that many individuals—perhaps even the majority of the world's population—are bilingual or multilingual. They must change tongue to go to work or school, to speak to elderly relatives, or deal with bureaucracy, making this **code-switching** a salient and significant part of their daily experience. In Africa, for example, it is common to switch between a small local language, a dominant regional language, and a former colonial language such as French, English, or

Portuguese. For immigrants to Europe there is switching between the family language and that of their new home—Turkish and German, or Arabic and French, for example.

The growth of English

Feelings of ownership, stereotyping, unequal distribution and power, individual and societal multilingualism—these are all issues at the heart of encounters between different languages, and have been so throughout history. They must be at the forefront of any applied linguistic investigation if it is to engage successfully with the many disputes which arise over the rights and relationships between languages, and the problem of how best to promote communication and understanding while also preserving cultural and linguistic identity. In a sense, there is nothing new about these matters. Similar issues to those which we confront today must have arisen, for example, in the Roman or Mogul empires. Yet there is also a sense in which recent years have witnessed a new phenomenon whose implications must be addressed by today's applied linguistics. Whereas, in the past, English was but one international language among others, it is now increasingly in a category of its own.

In addition to its four hundred million or so first-language speakers, and over a billion people who live in a country where it is an official language, English is now taught as the main foreign language in virtually every country, and used for business, education, and access to information by a substantial proportion of the world's population. Consequently the role of other international languages such as French or Russian has diminished drastically. As with geographical areas, so with areas of activity. French is no longer the international language of air traffic control, or dominant in diplomacy. German and Russian are no longer internationally necessary for scientific study. Nor is it just a question of native-speaker numbers. Although Putonghua remains the world's largest first language, it has not gained ground as either an official second language or a foreign language.

In recent years the growth of English has been further accelerated by a startling expansion in the quantity and speed of international communication. The rise of international corporations, linked to expanding US power and influence, ensures an ever-increasing use of English in business. Films, songs, television programmes, and advertisements in English are heard and seen in many countries where it is not the first nor even a second language, both feeding and reflecting this growth. The dominant language of the Internet is English, and, with the frequent absence of available software for writing systems other than the Roman alphabet, electronic mail is often conducted in English, even among people who share another language.

This new situation means that, for a large proportion of the world's population, the learning and use of English as an additional language is both a major language need—often one upon which their livelihood depends—and also one of the salient language experiences of their lives. In addition, both non-native and native speakers are involved in **Teaching English as a Foreign Language (TEFL)** as teachers, planners, administrators, publishers, and testers. For these reasons alone, the teaching and learning of English has generated tremendous personal, political, academic, and commercial interest. Accompanied (both as cause and effect) by globalization, and virtually unchallenged US military and economic ascendancy, the growth of English raises important concerns about the dangers of linguistic and cultural homogeneity. We shall turn to these in more detail in Chapter 6.

English and Englishes

This growth of English, however, also has some paradoxical consequences. Far from automatically extending the authority of English native speakers, it raises considerable doubts about whose language English is, and how judgements about it can be made. It may even—as we shall see shortly—make us reconsider not only our definition of 'English native speaker', but also whether this term is as significant in establishing norms for the language as is usually supposed.

As we observed at the beginning of this chapter, it is usual for speakers of a language, while welcoming the learning of it by others, to feel a sense of ownership towards it. In the case of smaller and less powerful languages, limited to a particular community in a particular place, this is both unexceptional and unremarkable. Once, however, a language begins to spread beyond its original homeland the situation changes and conflicts of opinion begin to emerge. Thus, even until surprisingly recently, many British English speakers regarded American English as an 'impure' deviation, rather as they might have regarded non-standard forms within their own islands. While such feelings of ownership are to be expected, they quickly become untenable when speakers of the 'offspring' variant become, as they are in the USA, more numerous and more internationally powerful than speakers of the 'parent'.

With any language which spreads this backwash effect is inevitable, and the justice of the process seems incontrovertible. There is a similar relationship between South American and Castilian Spanish, and the Portugueses of Brazil and Portugal. Yet despite the inevitability of this process, there is still possessiveness and attempts to call a halt. Few people nowadays would question the legitimacy of different standard **Englishes** for countries where it is the majority language. We talk of standard American English, standard Australian English, standard New Zealand English, and so on. Still contested by some, however, is the validity of standards for countries where, although English may be a substantial or official language, it is not that of the majority. Thus there is still opposition, even within the countries themselves, to the notion of Indian English, Singapore English, or Nigerian English. Far more contentious, however, is the possibility that, as English becomes more and more widely used, recognized varieties might emerge even in places where there is no national 'native speaker' population or official status. Could we, in the future, be talking about Dutch English, or Chinese English, or Mexican English?

The Indian scholar Braj Kachru describes this situation as one in which English exists in three concentric circles: the **inner circle** of the predominantly English-speaking countries; the **outer circle** of the former colonies where English is an official language; and the **expanding circle** where, although English is neither an official nor a former colonial language, it is increasingly part of many people's daily lives. At issue is the degree to which the English in each of these circles can provide legitimate descriptions and prescriptions. The rights of the outer circle are now reasonably well established. What, though, of the English used in the expanding circle? Could a new standard international English be emerging there, with its own rules and regularities, different from those of any of the 'native Englishes'?

Native speakers

All this raises issues about the very term **native speaker**. Let us pause for a moment to consider what is meant by it, and why it has become one of the most contentious in applied linguistics.

To do this, we need to look at some of the common assumptions about what it means to be a native speaker. Firstly, there is the question of personal history. Native speakers are considered to be people who acquired the language naturally and effortlessly in childhood, through a combination of exposure, the child's innate talent for language learning, and the need to communicate. Secondly, there is a question of expertise. Native speakers are seen as people who use the language, or a variety of it, correctly, and have insight into what is or is not acceptable. Thirdly, there is a question of knowledge and loyalty. Being a native speaker, it is assumed, entails knowledge of, and loyalty to, a community which uses the language.

In many cases this threefold definition is relatively unproblematic, particularly for small languages spoken mostly in one particular place. Take Icelandic for example, spoken by 300,000 Icelanders on an island of 100,000 square kilometres. Most people there have grown up speaking Icelandic, are expert in its use, and identify with Icelandic culture. In the case of larger and more widely distributed languages however, and most especially in the case of English, serious problems with the usual definitions of native speaker begin to emerge. Many English speakers— whether in the inner, outer, or expanding circle—grew up with and use another language in the home. Their cultural loyalty is wholly or partly to a non-English-speaking community and they may well be opposed to the dominant English-speaking culture, feeling that their own language and values are threatened.

None of this, however, necessarily reflects upon their expertise. Many such English speakers use the language just as expertly as the traditionally defined native speakers. Certainly there are often—though by no means always—minor differences of accent, phrasing, or confidence in grammaticality judgements. Yet these are just as often accompanied by additional expertise which a traditionally defined native speaker may not have.

Here it is important to take stock of those aspects of language proficiency which the traditional definition of the native speaker does *not* include. Firstly, it says nothing about proficiency in writing, but only about proficiency in speech. Indeed, some native speakers are illiterate, and many of those who can write do so inaccurately ('Lovly new potato's') or clumsily ('Revised customer service arrangements presently under implementation'). Secondly, the native speaker's knowledge of the language is implicit rather than explicit. He or she uses the rules correctly, in other words, but cannot necessarily explain them. For example, try asking the average native speaker to explain the difference between 'shall' and 'will'. Lastly, traditional native speakerness implies nothing about size of vocabulary, range of styles, or ability to communicate across diverse communities. In all of these aspects of proficiency, it is quite common to find that the expertise of the non-native speaker exceeds that of many native speakers.

English as a Lingua Franca (ELF)

In addition, these highly proficient users of English are not necessarily aspiring to speak any of the standard Englishes from either the inner or the outer circles. Rather, there is a strong case for saying that they speak a new variety of English which depends neither on childhood acquisition nor on cultural identity, and is often used in communication in which no native speaker is involved. This is often referred to as **English as a Lingua Franca (ELF)**. What matters in its use is clarity and comprehensibility rather than conformity to one of the existing standards. Indeed, being a native speaker in the traditional sense does not necessarily imply expertise in ELF, and for the purposes of international communication native speakers may need to adjust their language to a new norm.

This rapid growth of ELF should be a major concern to contemporary applied linguistics if it is to live up to the definition offered in Chapter 1. There is an urgent need for documentation and analysis of the world's changing language landscape, and for informed advice. We need to consider whether the current situation is unprecedented, whether it has produced a new set of language related problems (whether, for example, the spread of international English is implicated in the decline and disappearance of other languages and, if so, how this should affect language planning). These are pressing issues, affecting in one way or another everyone who learns or uses English, native and non-native speaker alike.

Considerable insight into changes in the distribution of English, and our attitudes to its use, can be gained by tracing the history of **English Language Teaching (ELT)** through the twentieth century. Different approaches to teaching English did not just occur by chance, but in response to changing geopolitical circumstances and social attitudes and values, as well as to shifts of fashion in linguistics which, for all its apparent objectivity, was itself subject to social change. Thus each successive movement in ELT has had its own particular stance on language and language learning, and on what English is, reflecting the ideology of its time. Changes in the distribution and balance of languages, and in particular the growth of ELF, have both reflected and influenced the populations and purposes of language learners. It is within this broader context that we now go on, in the next chapter, to trace the development of ELT.

4

English Language Teaching (ELT)

The spread of English described in the last chapter, and the related expansion of its use and learning, have generated intense interest in how and whether it is possible to improve the results of English teaching, and consequently in the study of language pedagogy and of **Second-Language Acquisition (SLA)**. Historically, the most active of applied linguistic enquiry has been in these areas. Indeed, in the early days of the discipline, applied linguistics and the study of **Teaching English as a Foreign Language (TEFL)** were considered to be one and the same.

The insights from this area of study, however, have a far wider relevance than might at first appear. Investigating language learning inevitably entails, in a particularly focused way, debate about what knowing and using a language actually means. At the same time it promotes understanding of the relationship between individual experience, social change, and abstract theories, which lies at the heart of all applied linguistic study. Consequently, ideas initially developed in relation to TEFL can inform approaches to a far wider range of applied linguistic concerns than they did in the past. However, before we develop this theme, we need first to look back at the development of TEFL over the last hundred or so years.

Grammar-translation language teaching

In the schoolrooms of Europe at the close of the nineteenth century, the teaching of modern foreign languages was heavily influenced by the more established and prestigious academic study of the dead classical languages, Latin and Ancient Greek.

Curriculum aims were largely a matter of consensus, and thus seldom spelled out as they would be today. Modern language learning, it was assumed, brought students into contact with the great national civilizations and their literatures. It trained minds in logical thought, developed elegant expression, and perpetuated the study of the language as an academic discipline. The best—if inimitable—examples of the language were its greatest writers: Shakespeare for English, Dante for Italian, Pushkin for Russian, and so forth.

In the daily grind of the schoolroom, however, these lofty aspirations seemed very distant. Uses of the language, if thought about at all, were deferred to the time when school or university would be completed. In the meantime, grammar rules were explained to the students in their own language, vocabulary lists were learned with translation equivalents, and then sentences—especially constructed to contain only the grammar and vocabulary which had already been covered—were laboriously translated, in writing, into and out of the student's first language. Such sentences, often bizarrely remote from any conceivable use, have been the occasion for jokes ever since. We have probably all heard references to the apocryphal 'My postilion has been struck by lightning' and the infamous '*plume de ma tante*'. The phonetician Henry Sweet, a leading opponent of **grammar-translation** language teaching, described them as 'a bag into which grammar and vocabulary are crammed without regard to meaning' and provided his own parody: 'The merchant is swimming with the gardener's son, but the Dutchman has the fine gun'.

Joking apart, however, we should take note of grammar-translation's assumptions about language learning, if only because they were so thoroughly rejected in later years and can thus provide a key insight into ways in which ideas about languages and language learning have changed. In this 'traditional' language teaching, the way into the new language was always through the student's own first language. Complicated rules were mastered and this mastery then tested by means of translation. Success was measured in terms of the accurate use of grammar and vocabulary rather than effective communication. (No marks for saying 'Me go sleep now' when you are tired and want to go to bed!) Using the language meant written translation. There was no emphasis on the development of fluent speech: it was better to get things right slowly than say them fast and effectively, but incorrectly. It was assumed that the processes of learning the language and eventual use of it could be disassociated. Eventually, perhaps, for some students anyway, one would lead to the other, but the ends were most definitely different from the means.

The direct method

At the turn of the nineteenth and twentieth centuries grammar-translation was in its heyday, especially in the privileged secondary schools of Europe. Yet, at the very same time, language-learning populations were already changing in ways which were to gather momentum throughout the twentieth century. For example, in the early years of the century there was continuing mass immigration, by speakers of many different languages, into the USA—a country whose unity has depended upon the use of English even though, to this day, it has no official language! And throughout the century, despite the interruptions of two world wars, there was growing international trade and tourism and an increase in both vocational and recreational language learning.

New types of students—immigrants, business people, and tourists—created a new kind of classroom population. In the language schools and evening classes which catered for them, the students did not necessarily share the same first language, making it simply impossible for instruction to proceed through first-language explanation and translation. In addition, the new type of student needed spoken as well as written language, and they needed it fast.

Language-learning experts (they were not then called applied linguists) responded to this challenge with radical new ideas about how languages should be taught. They advocated a **direct method** in which the students' own languages were banished and everything was to be done through the language under instruction. Translation and first-language explanation were banned and the new method enforced, sometimes quite ruthlessly. In the highly successful Berlitz Schools, for example, classroom microphones monitored what teachers were saying, and they could be fired for uttering a single word in a student's own language. In many ways the direct method classroom, by insisting on one language and outlawing bilingualism, emulated the most repressive of monolingual nations.

The direct method established a concept of language learning very different from that implicit in grammar-translation. Knowledge of a language was no longer an object of scholarship attainable simply by hard work. Success was to be measured instead by the degree to which the learner's language proficiency approximated to that of the native speaker, a goal which was not at that time seen as problematic. This led the way to further changes in both popular and applied linguistics ideas about how a language might be learned.

'Natural' language learning

The early direct method had been a revolution, but not a complete one. Many of the characteristics of grammar-translation had survived. There was still explanation and grading of grammar rules, and the language was divided into discrete areas such as vocabulary or pronunciation practice. Teachers, then, had to do much as they had done before, but without recourse to either first-language explanation or translation. This meant that, in practice, grammar rules had to be worked out by students from examples, because an explanation would demand language beyond the level of the rule being explained, while the meaning of new vocabulary had to be either guessable from the context, or perhaps illustrated or mimed. This last resort is possible, if often ridiculous, for a word denoting something specific and physical, like 'butterfly'— but imagine the plight of teachers trying to mime more general words such as 'creature' or abstract ones such as 'specification'!

In the 1970s and 1980s, however, these endemic problems of the direct method were bypassed by radical 'new' ideas. The so-called **natural approach** revived the notion—previously promulgated under exactly the same name in the nineteenth century!—that an adult learner can repeat the route to proficiency of the native-speaking child. The idea was that learning would take place without explanation or grading, and without correction of errors, but simply by exposure to 'meaningful input'. This approach was based upon theorizing and research in SLA which purported to show that learners, whatever their first language, would follow an internally determined natural order of their own, and that neither explicit instruction nor conscious learning had any effect.

In many ways, the natural approach is an object lesson in what applied linguistics should not be. For it sought to impose upon teachers, without consultation and without consideration for their existing practices and beliefs, ideas based upon academic research and theorizing. Its view of SLA, moreover, was derived directly from mainstream linguistics research into child first-language acquisition, where the early stages are largely internally driven and impervious to instruction. This research was then assumed to be directly relevant—indeed imperative—to changes in the way languages were taught. In addition, the approach was culturally insensitive: it was developed in the USA and then exported as globally relevant without regard to differing educational traditions or language-learning contexts. It paid no heed, for example, to variations in class size or to concepts of teacher role. Most damning of all, however, is the fact that the research on which it was based is seriously flawed in that instruction *does* effect learning and there *are* variations depending on the language being learned. A cautionary tale indeed!

The natural approach, with its suggestion that learning need not involve hard work, was superficially seductive and there is no doubt that it attracted many followers in its day. While now seldom followed in its extreme form, it continues to exert a considerable influence. Conscious learning, correction of errors, practice activities, and attention to form are all kept at arm's length, only readmitted with some reluctance and disdain, while what are perceived as their opposites—'natural' and 'meaningful' and 'real' activities—retain something of a sacred aura.

The communicative approach

At roughly the same time as the development of the natural approach, there emerged a far more durable new movement known as the **communicative approach** or **Communicative Language Teaching (CLT)**, which rapidly became, and still remains, the dominant orthodoxy in progressive language teaching. The theories behind it have had a profound and far-reaching effect, not only in language teaching but in many other applied linguistic areas too.

In practice, both CLT and the natural approach can lead to similar meaning-focused activities and for this reason they have often been confused. The resemblance, however, is superficial, for their underlying rationales are deeply opposed. The focus of CLT was primarily and necessarily social, concerned as it was with the goal of successful communication. In contrast, the natural approach was essentially psychological, based upon the idea, derived from first-language acquisition studies, that attention to meaning would somehow trigger the natural cognitive development of the language system.

The essence of CLT is a shift of attention from the language system as end in itself to the successful use of that system in context; that is to say from an emphasis on form to an emphasis on communication. Language-learning success is to be assessed neither in terms of accurate grammar and pronunciation for their own sake, nor in terms of explicit knowledge of the rules, but by the ability to *do* things with the language, appropriately, fluently, and effectively. Consequently communicative pedagogy shifted its attention from the teaching and practice of grammar and pronunciation rules, and the learning of vocabulary lists, to communicative activities.

As pointed out at the time by its more thoughtful advocates, accurate use of the language system remained the major resource for successful communication. The richer strands of the CLT movement were not therefore advocating the abandonment of attention to form, as advocates of the natural approach were, but rather two changes of emphasis. The first was that, in addition to mastery of form, learners need other kinds of ability and knowledge if they are to communicate successfully. The second was that forms should be approached in the context of their usefulness rather than as an end in themselves. In other words, the traditional sequence of language learning was reversed. Whereas in the past, whether in grammar-translation or in direct method teaching, the emphasis had been upon mastery of forms first and their use later, CLT students considered first what they needed to do with the language and then learned the forms which would fulfil those needs. Teachers and materials designers were urged to identify things learners need to do with the language (i.e. conduct a **needs analysis**) and simulate these in the classroom. This, it was believed, would also motivate the learners by constantly emphasizing the relevance of classroom activity to their goals.

This shift of emphasis from the means to the ends of language learning has had far-reaching consequences at both the macro level of syllabus and curriculum design and at the micro level of classroom activity. At the macro level, there has been the development of language for specific purposes (in the case of English, **English for Specific Purposes (ESP)**) which tries to develop the language and discourse skills which will be needed for particular jobs (English for Occupational Purposes (EOP)) or for particular fields of study (English for Academic Purposes (EAP)). At the micro level there has been the development of **Task-Based Instruction (TBI)**, in which learning is organized around tasks related to real-world activities, focusing the student's attention upon meaning and upon successful task completion. While the rationale for ESP is entirely social, working back from student objectives in the outside world to syllabus content, TBI attempts to unite this perspective with one which is also **psycholinguistic**. Its argument, based on SLA research findings, is that the keys to acquisition are attention to meaning rather than form, negotiation with another speaker, and the motivation created by real-world relevance. In this respect TBI is in direct line of descent from both the natural and the communicative approaches.

All of these developments of the communicative approach differ markedly from the various kinds of teaching which preceded them. While, in traditional approaches, the emphasis was on formal practice, and elements of the language system were isolated and taught step by step, in CLT the emphasis became quite different. Language, it was argued, is best handled all at once, as it would be in the real world, as this is the learner's ultimate goal. Consequently there is little point in breaking things down artificially—better to get started straight away.

This, at least, was the ideal. In practice, as has often since been pointed out, communicative activities could lead to limited proficiency and a constraining and conformist model of language use. Thus, at its worst, emphasis on functions rather than forms could degenerate into learning phrase-book-like lists of things to say in particular situations. Concentration upon communicating meaning from the outset could lead to inaccurate—if temporarily successful—language use which, uncorrected, could then fossilize, preventing the learner from further development for more complex use. The focus upon ends was, in practice, interpreted in a utilitarian way, seeing work and the transaction of mundane information as the limit of the learner's needs, thus denying attention to the aesthetic, playful, and creative aspects of language use, and its role in creating and maintaining relationships. Above all, the belief that communication would be aided by situationally and culturally appropriate use of the language was often rather thoughtlessly interpreted to mean that the foreign learner of English should conform to the norms and conventions of an English-speaking community. The sum of all of these limitations was the denial to learners of the resources needed to develop a creative command of the language which would enable them to express their own individual and social meanings. Ironically, the communicative approach could often stifle rather than promote the richest kinds of communication.

This well-documented slippage between theory and practice illustrates a particular kind of applied linguistic problem. It also emphasizes the importance of considering more closely an issue which is at the heart of all applied linguistic enquiry: what it means to learn, to know, and to use a language. To examine this problem and to extend our discussion of areas other than language teaching, we will benefit from closer assessment of the theory from which CLT derives, and it is to this that we turn in the next chapter.

Before moving on, however, it is worth spelling out some general lessons to be learned from this present chapter's history of changing ELT fashions. Here we have a clear and classic applied linguistic problem—how best to teach and learn a language. Yet instead of one single answer we have a host of very different and sharply opposed points of view. Why all this confusion and contradiction?

There are perhaps a number of reasons. It is clear that changes in approaches to teaching have no single cause. They come about partly in response to changing perceptions of 'good' language use, partly in response to developments in linguistics, and partly in response to changing political and demographic circumstances. Success in language learning, moreover, is not an absolute category. It varies with the values of the age and with many other factors besides, for example, what the language is to be used for, by whom, and in what circumstances. Answers to applied linguistics problems, in other words, if this one is anything to go by, are not likely to be stable, final, or value-free.

The error comes, though, when those approaching such problems do so with dogmatic certainty, taking the perspectives and values of their own time and place as the only ones which can ever apply. To combat such dogmatism, and to counter unthinking fads and fashions, a great deal is to be gained, in ELT as in other areas of activity, by placing problems in a wider historical and cultural perspective. By doing this, applied linguistics can make a crucially valuable contribution to debate.

5
Language and communication

Knowing a language

What does it mean to know a language well and to use it successfully? Answers to this question vary considerably, both historically and culturally, and between individuals. They, also, as we are beginning to see, depend on the perspective of the person who is being asked the question: for example, an academic linguist, a language user, or a language learner. Does knowing a language imply native-speaker insight and fluency? An ability to produce sentences with no grammatical errors? The capacity to write elegantly and expressively? Being able to get your meanings across and do what you need to do? Or is it a combination of these? Which answer we choose will profoundly affect how we address any problem in which language is implicated.

Traditional grammar-translation language teaching, which we considered in Chapter 4, assumed that knowing the rules of a language and being able to use them were one and the same thing. Yet there are many cases where someone knows the rules of a language but is still not a successful communicator. They may, for example, not use the language fast enough. Or they may understand what is being said and have something to say themselves, but still somehow fail to join in. Or perhaps their language seems stilted and old-fashioned, for example, they may say things like 'Whom do you want?' or 'It's raining cats and dogs'. Or they may send the wrong kinds of signals with their body and tone of voice, shaking their head instead of nodding it, sounding bored or unfriendly when they do not intend to. Or they may understand the literal meaning of what is said, but not why it is said. They fail to realize that something is a joke, for example, and take offence.

In other words, knowing the grammar and vocabulary of the language, although essential, is one thing. Being able to put them to use involves other types of knowledge and ability as well.

Linguistic competence

Despite this rather obvious point, isolating the formal systems of language (i.e. its pronunciation, grammar, and vocabulary) either for learning or for analysis, is a useful first step. However, the adoption of traditional language-teaching methods need not imply that this is all that learning a language involves, but only that a sound knowledge of the rules and an accurate, if slow, deployment of them is the basis for further development. In other words, an emphasis on formal correctness can be seen as a matter of pedagogic procedure, a strategic staging of information, of the kind which is familiar in any kind of ordered learning. You do not learn to drive by going straight into high-speed traffic for example, but by first practising isolated operations and listening to someone explain what to do.

A more fundamental, and rather different, argument for separating the formal systems of a language from other kinds of knowledge and skills has come from theoretical linguistics, and in particular the work of Noam Chomsky, described in Chapter 1. We need to take further account of his ideas because they have been so extraordinarily influential in all areas of language study. A good deal of applied linguistic work has either followed on from them, or defined itself in opposition to them.

Chomsky's idea is that the human capacity for language, as illustrated by a child's acquisition of the language around them, is not the product of general intelligence or learning ability, but an innate, genetically determined feature of the human species. We are born with considerable pre-programmed knowledge of how language works, and require only minimal exposure to activate our connection to the particular language around us—rather as a bird learning to fly adapts to the environment outside the nest. In this view, the newborn infant brain already contains a **Universal Grammar (UG)** which forms the basis of competence in the particular language the child goes on to speak. This **linguistic competence** is seen as modular, that is to say separate from other mental abilities.

If we accept Chomsky's view, language, as an object of academic enquiry, becomes something more biological than social, and similarities between languages outweigh differences. In addition, language is separated from other factors involved in its use such as body language or cultural knowledge. While this view may be valid for certain purposes in linguistics it also means that Chomsky's theories, when invoked in applied linguistics, can have a reductive and constraining effect, excluding from consideration those very factors with which the discipline is most concerned.

Communicative competence

Saying there is more to using a language than knowing the grammar is relatively easy. Formulating precisely what other kinds of knowledge are involved is more complicated. An influential attempt to do this was made by the sociolinguist Dell Hymes in his description of **communicative competence** in the late 1960s. The term is offered as a deliberate contrast to Chomsky's linguistic competence. As Hymes observes, a person who had only linguistic competence would be quite unable to communicate. They would be a kind of social monster producing grammatical sentences unconnected to the situation in which they occur. What is needed for successful communication, Hymes suggested, is four types of knowledge: **possibility**, **feasibility**, **appropriateness**, and **attestedness**. Let us consider each in turn.

Firstly, a communicatively competent speaker knows what is formally possible in a language, i.e. whether an instance conforms to the rules of grammar and pronunciation. They know, for example, that 'Me go sleep now' transgresses these rules, while 'I am going to go to sleep now' does not. Knowledge of possibility is not sufficient in itself for communication. 'I am going to sleep now' may be grammatical, meaningful, and correctly pronounced, but it is not necessarily the 'right' thing to say, whereas 'Me go sleep now', although 'wrong', may be both meaningful and appropriate. In addition, a communicatively competent speaker may know the rules, be capable of following them, but nevertheless break them deliberately. This is often the case when people want to be witty, or creative, or intimate, or to talk about something for which the language has no existing terms. Thus, for example, the Beatle Ringo Starr, after working long hours on a film set, remarked 'That was a hard day's night', and the phrase was taken up as the title of a song and a film. Though it breaks semantic rules, it expresses an idea very effectively.

Secondly, a communicatively competent person knows what is feasible. This is a psychological concept concerned with limitations to what can be processed by the mind, and is best illustrated by an example. The rules of English grammar make it possible to expand a noun phrase, and make it more specific, by adding a relative clause. Thus 'the cheese' can become 'the cheese the rat ate'. Likewise, 'the rat' can become 'the rat the cat chased'. In theory, this should allow us to expand a sentence infinitely as follows:

The cheese was green.
The cheese the rat ate was green.
The cheese the rat the cat chased ate was green.
The cheese the rat the cat the dog saw chased ate was green.
The cheese the rat the cat the dog the man beat saw chased ate was green.

These last two sentences, however, are hardly ones that would work in communication. If anything, they seem clumsier than an 'impossible' example like 'Me go sleep now'. They may be possible, in other words, but they are not feasible. They do not work, not because they are ungrammatical, but because they are so difficult to process.

The notion of feasibility may seem a rather academic one, and of little relevance to the practical applications of knowledge about language. Processing the convoluted sentence about the cheese and the rat is more like a game than a real-world problem.

Feasibility does nevertheless have some important consequences for applied linguistics. It bears upon the important issue of making information easily accessible, which in the modern world, with its overload of information, is particularly important. Consider, for example, the following legal sentence:

> If a premium remains in default after the end of its grace period, any cash surrender value of the Policy will be used to continue the Policy in force as paid up insurance or as extended term insurance, in an amount as determined below, and no further premiums will be due.

We might want to criticize it not on the grounds that it is ungrammatical, but rather on the grounds that it is not very feasible and thus unnecessarily obscures important information. This is a topic to which we shall return in Chapter 7.

A third component of communicative competence is knowledge of appropriateness. This concerns the relationship of language or behaviour to context, and as such covers a wide range of phenomena. Its importance is clear if we consider its opposite, inappropriateness. Something might be, for example, inappropriate to a particular relationship (calling a police officer 'darling' or tickling them as they reprimand you); to a particular kind of text (using slang or taboo words in a formal letter); to a particular situation (answering a mobile phone call during a funeral); or generally inappropriate to a particular culture (not showing deference to the elderly).

Appropriateness concerns conformity to social convention, and as such is fraught with controversy. Perhaps this is easiest to see in non-verbal communication. Take, for example, the issue of appropriate dress for women moving between Western and Islamic cultures. One point of view is that maintaining the norms of one society is inappropriate in the other. Thus European women visiting the Gulf States are advised to wear long sleeves and long skirts to avoid giving offence. Moslem women, visiting or living in the West, may feel under pressure to stop covering their heads. Very often this may be a matter for individual decision making, but there are occasions when it spills over into the public domain and a society seeks to impose its own norms. People feel very strongly about such issues and there are arguments on both sides. Important factors are the degree to which some values are perceived to be absolute rather than culture specific, for example, religious freedom, female modesty, and women's rights; the degree to which a society should respect ethnic difference among its members; and the degree to which visitors should conform to the etiquette of their hosts.

Such issues, although easier to see in non-verbal behaviour, also arise in language use. Should learners of a language necessarily adopt the way in which it is used? Can Japanese speakers, for example, maintain the deferential politeness of their own culture, even when speaking English? Should Arabic speakers drop all reference to God in their English, making it 'inappropriate' for example, to say 'If God is willing' in answer to an enquiry about whether something is likely to happen? Such culture clashes can occur, even between speakers of the same language. Many speakers of British English find phrases used in US service encounters effusive and false, for example, 'Have a nice day' and 'Your call matters to us'. Conversely, many speakers of American English find the language—if any—used in such encounters in Britain curt and unfriendly.

For applied linguists there is no avoiding such issues. Language creates our identities and allows us to communicate with others. Its study must be concerned with who imposes upon whom, and with the limits of social coercion and dissent. Many activities, for example, schooling, workplace communication, language therapy, language testing, and language planning, are essentially concerned with negotiating the parameters of difference and conformity. And in the modern world, where formerly distinct ways of living are brought increasingly into sharp contact, and people from different cultures have to share the same space, these issues are becoming urgent.

Hymes' fourth component of communicative competence is knowledge of attestedness, i.e. 'whether ... something is done'. At first glance, this seems rather puzzling. Surely occurrence can be accounted for by the other three parameters? This is not, however, necessarily the case. Take, for example, the phrase 'chips and fish'. From one point of view this is possible (it does not break any grammar rule), feasible (it is easily processed and readily understandable), and appropriate (it does not contravene any sensitive social convention). Nevertheless, it does not occur as frequently as 'fish and chips'. In the 1970s, when Hymes' ideas first attracted attention, there was no easy way to say what uses did actually occur other than by laborious checking of texts and transcripts. More recently, **corpus linguistics** (see Chapter 8), which uses computerized techniques for searching large databanks, has made available much more information about probability.

The influence of communicative competence

Directly or indirectly, the notion of communicative competence has been very widely drawn upon in all areas of applied linguistics. In first-language education—the area which Hymes was, in fact, addressing—it was invoked to justify a shift away from developing only mechanical language skills towards a more rounded capacity to communicate, a trend which has now largely been reversed. In information design, for example, the drafting of official documents and forms, it supported the view that stating facts is not enough, they also need to be easily accessible. In speech therapy it justified an increased emphasis on social knowledge and skills in addition to deficiencies in grammar and pronunciation. In translation it strengthened the case for seeking an equivalent effect rather than only formal and literal equivalence.

The biggest single influence however, as is so often the case in applied linguistics, has been upon the teaching of English as a foreign language. Inspired by Hymes, the **communicative approach**, which we looked at in Chapter 4, aimed to develop learners' capacity to use the language effectively. Given the narrowness of the methods which preceded it, with their excessive emphasis upon grammatical accuracy, this approach should have been beneficial, allowing teachers and learners to achieve a more balanced view of what successful communication involves. Yet despite the careful advice of those applied linguists who introduced Hymes' ideas to the language-teaching profession, the idea quickly became distorted and misinterpreted. The four parameters of Hymes' model were not taken as integral parts of a complex model of communication but rather as discrete areas to be developed separately. They were even set against each other, with a focus on appropriateness, in particular, being seen as a replacement for one on possibility. Nor was there interpretation and adjustment to different contexts and for different learners. In the haste to exploit the concept commercially, the crucial applied linguistics processes by which theory is reinterpreted for, and by, practice, were neglected.

There were a number of contributory factors. Some advocates of the communicative approach found common cause with the so-called 'natural' approach and the idea, described in Chapter 4, that the foreign-language learner can repeat the child's acquisition of language through use and exposure alone. In this version of CLT, the emphasis did not really shift away from grammar as the sole yardstick of success; there was just a different route to attaining that end.

In addition, CLT often over-reacted against the past. The new emphasis, mentioned above, was almost exclusively upon appropriateness, while the other elements of communicative competence received little attention. Focus upon what is possible was rejected as old-fashioned, while the notions of feasibility and attestedness, being more difficult to grasp, had little or no impact.

In many materials, moreover, the notion of appropriateness became distorted. There was an implicit assumption that someone learning English should abandon their own ways of behaving and the English language became a vehicle for promoting certain aspects of British and US culture. For example, the typical language learner was presented as an affluent youthful visitor who wanted nothing more than to fit in with the right way of doing things in Britain or the USA as quickly as possible. A typical 'communicative' activity might involve simulating the successful ordering of a meal in a restaurant in London or New York, or knowing how to make polite requests and apologies at a party.

While this suited publishers producing courses for an affluent global market, it often disempowered certain types of learner. The potential for other cultures to have an impact on English, or for learners to develop separate identities within it, was neglected. Little heed was taken, for example, of the needs of immigrants and members of ethnic minorities who might wish, quite legitimately, both to belong to their new society and to maintain their original identity.

This last development is ironic. One of the strengths of the concept of communicative competence is that it does not assume that knowledge necessarily leads to conformity. Knowing what is appropriate to a particular situation, relationship, genre, or culture, does not mean that you necessarily do it. There are many instances where people depart from the norm. They may wish to dissent from the conventional values of a society, to assert those of another, or to be humorous, creative, rude, or aggressive. There are in short good reasons why people do not conform— but in order to communicate the meanings they create by these departures, they need first to know what the norms are.

The fate of the concept of communicative competence is an object lesson for applied linguistics. It shows how, when transferred to a practical domain, theories and descriptions of language use, however powerful, quickly become simplified and fall victim to vested interests. Ideas which are to survive this fate need to take these forces into account and build the likely impact of the outside world into their very structure. They need to take account of language as a lived experience rather than only as an object of academic study.

Communicative competence remains, however, an extremely powerful model for applied linguistics, not only in language teaching but in every area of enquiry. It moves beyond the rarefied atmospheres of theoretical linguistics and traditional language teaching, and, while itself also an idealized model, can aid the process of referring linguistic abstraction back to the actuality from which it is derived.

It has also contributed to a growing interest in the analysis of language use, not only as a source of examples illustrating an underlying system but also as social action with important effects both at the micro level of personal experience and at the macro level of social change. In particular the notion of appropriateness, by emphasizing how successful language use varies with context, stimulated applied linguistic interest in two areas of enquiry—discourse analysis and cross-cultural communication. Quite why these are so important to applied linguistics we shall see in Chapter 6.

6
Context and culture

For its users, instances of language are never abstracted, they always happen in specific situations. They belong to particular people and are used to realize those people's purposes. In linguistics, however, language is very obviously abstracted from experience in order to be better understood as a system, enabling grammatical regularities to be seen more clearly, even perhaps providing an insight into the representation of language in the mind. For applied linguistics, such analyses of language are relevant to understanding the experience of language in use, but they must be combined with another kind of analysis too.

Communicative competence, as observed at the end of Chapter 5, is also in its way an abstraction. In the actual experience of language its four parameters are neither as discrete nor as static as the model is sometimes taken to suggest. Yet it is a different kind of abstraction from descriptions of the formal systems of grammar and sound, and it views language from a different perspective. It points the way towards the analysis of language in use, enabling us to take into account many relevant factors other than the words themselves.

These other factors are many. All of the following, for example, might be involved in interpreting a real encounter: tone of voice and facial expression; the relationship between speakers; their age, sex, and social status; the time and place; and the degree to which speakers do—or do not—share the same cultural background. Collectively, such factors are known as **context**, and they are all relevant to whether a particular action or utterance is, to use Hymes' term, appropriate. As applied linguistics necessarily engages with the use of language, they must be central to any analysis. In this chapter we consider how context, and in particular cultural context, can be analysed and understood, and in general terms how it is relevant to all the areas of applied linguistics. In the latter part of the chapter we focus, in particular, upon the practice of translation.

Systematizing context: discourse analysis

Systematic description of context is notoriously difficult. It threatens to introduce enormous amounts of new material, and categories which are inherently slippery and vague. These are reasons for caution, but not for retreat. It is not the case, as some linguists have claimed, that the meaning of language in context is so messy and subjective that it is beyond the reach of systematic enquiry. To demonstrate this, applied linguistics has drawn upon, and also developed, **discourse analysis**—the study of how stretches of language in context are perceived as meaningful and unified by their users. Three areas of study which contribute to this field are paralanguage, pragmatics, and genre studies. Let us deal, briefly, with each of these in turn.

When we speak we do not only communicate through words. A good deal is conveyed by tone of voice—whether we shout or whisper for example, and by the use of our bodies—whether we smile, wave our hands, touch people, make eye contact, and so on. Such communicative behaviour, used alongside language, is **paralanguage**. Convincing research suggests that paralinguistic messages can outweigh linguistic ones, especially in establishing and maintaining relationships. For this reason, understanding of paralanguage is relevant in any professional activity involved with effective communication, or developing effective communication in others, such as media training, speech therapy, and language teaching.

Writing has paralanguage too. Written words can be scribbled, printed, or painted, and their meaning can be amplified or altered by layout, accompanying pictures, and diagrams. New technologies make the paralanguage of writing increasingly more significant, for whereas, in the past, resources were limited to handwriting, typing, or printing, the computer has brought powerful new tools for document design within many people's reach.

Indeed, whether written, spoken, or a mixture of the two, language cannot be used for communication without paralanguage. We must use *some* facial expression when we speak or make *some* choice of script or font when we write. Yet, curiously, considering this inextricable involvement in communication, paralanguage has not been extensively studied by applied linguists. Its role in speech has been left to psychology, and in writing to typography and information design. At a time when new technologies mix writing and visual effects in ways which may be altering fundamentally the nature and process of communication, there is a pressing need to integrate findings from these disparate areas. The study of **visual communication** and **Computer-Mediated Communication (CMC)** are growing areas in applied linguistics, and likely to be increasingly important in the future.

Pragmatics is the discipline which studies the knowledge and procedures which enable people to understand each other's words. Its main concern is not the literal meaning, but what speakers intend to do with their words and what it is which makes this intention clear. Consider, for example, a simple and familiar utterance such as 'How are you?' Grammatically, it is an interrogative English sentence; taken literally, it is a question about someone's health. It can also—more typically—be a greeting, to be answered reciprocally along the lines of 'Fine thanks, how are you?' Yet it could also, depending on context, take on many other meanings besides. It might be answered, for example, by any of the following: 'Mind your own business' (rejecting a stranger's unwanted attentions); 'Don't make me sick' (rebutting overtures after an argument); 'Deeply depressed' (reflecting on a recent bereavement); or 'Thanks be to God' (seeking to convey Islamic culture when speaking English). Meaning, in other words, varies with circumstances and it is easy to think of situations in which all of these responses might be both effective and appropriate.

Meaning also changes with the kind of communicative event to which words belong. You might describe the same person very differently, for example, when gossiping about them, writing a job reference, introducing them to a friend, or giving a funeral oration after their death. Events of this kind are described as

genres, a term defined by the applied linguist John Swales as a class of communicative events which share some set of communicative purposes. Other possible examples of genres include conversations, consultations, lessons, emails, Web pages, brochures, prayers, news bulletins, stories, jokes, operas, and soap operas. Any instance of communication belongs to one category of genre or another, or perhaps to a mixture of several.

All these elements of discourse—interpreting paralanguage, understanding pragmatic intention, and distinguishing different genres—are part of a person's communicative competence, integral to their use and understanding of language. For this reason, discourse analysis is crucial to applied linguistic analysis in areas involving the development or assessment of language proficiency (for example, language education, speech therapy, and language testing), and successful communication (for example, workplace communication, translation, and information design).

Culture

The successful interpretation of language in context depends upon the degree to which the participants share conventions and procedures, including those related to paralanguage, pragmatics, and genre. Such conventions and procedures, together with the values and beliefs which lie behind them, are elements of cultural knowledge, and the people who share them can be thought of as belonging to the same culture. **Cross-cultural communication** between members of different national or ethnic communities is likely to be involved in every area of applied linguistic activity. In some, for example, language planning, foreign language education, and translation, it is intrinsic—they are, of their nature, about it. In others, while not intrinsic, it is very likely to be involved given the multicultural nature of contemporary societies. Clinical linguistics, for example, frequently deals with individuals whose communication needs involve more than one language and more than one set of cultural procedures. And language use in the workplace and the law courts, and for marketing or information, inevitably involves members of different communities.

Defined in this conventional sense, cross-cultural communication is central to our concerns. Yet there is also a broader sense in which, even within communities, communication across different groups with different knowledge and values can be conceived of as being cross-cultural. Examples include generations, social classes, the two sexes, and different sexual orientations. In fact communication and the problems which surround it, and therefore applied linguistics itself, is in many ways an inherently cross-cultural phenomenon.

As with languages, there is disagreement over the degree to which cultures, for all their obvious disparity, reflect universal human attributes. Some argue that the differences are superficial and that cultural conventions everywhere realize the same basic human needs. In this view, apparent variation masks underlying similarity. Greeting conventions for example—kissing, bowing, pressing palms, or shaking hands—may all appear to be very different, but have in common the use of the body to communicate degrees of intimacy and power.

Yet, as with language, there is a disparity between academic theorizing about cultural universals and lived experience. Whatever the degree of underlying similarity, it is the differences which are often most salient in cross-cultural encounters. When a language is not shared, there is a straightforward and very apparent barrier to communication. With cultural conventions, however, the consequences may be less apparent but more damaging. There is not only an absence of understanding, but potential for misunderstanding too. In some cultures a nod of the head means 'yes' while in others virtually the same gesture means 'no'. People used to routine physical contact with acquaintances—kissing as a greeting for example—may judge those who are not so demonstrative as unfriendly or cold. Those accustomed to silence in deference to higher status may see more garrulous cultures as pushy and insensitive. The same customs, in other words, can send quite different signals, with potentially disastrous results for cross-cultural understanding. One major role for applied linguistics is to raise awareness of the degree to which the meaning of behaviour is culturally relative, thus combating prejudice, and contributing to the improvement of community relations and conflict resolution in general.

Yet whether we choose to emphasize commonality or difference, it would be wrong to regard cultures as either static or neatly bounded. They are constantly changing and leaking at the boundaries. In Britain, for example, over the last fifty years or so, there have been many changes in convention which reflect changes in underlying relationships. In greeting conventions kissing has become commonplace (though not between men) and the use of first names (rather than title and surname) has increased. So there is variation across time and permeation from other traditions. It is hard to generalize or make fixed descriptions.

In a similar way, it is an oversimplification to equate culture with nationality, using terms such as 'Brazilian culture' and 'Turkish culture'. Such labels overlook the cultural variation within nations of social class, ethnicity, age, education, and individual preference. In modern societies, cultural identity is often multivalent, an intersection of many different loyalties and influences of which nationality is only one. In addition, increased migration means that a growing number of people have links to two or more nations, although—precisely because a dominant factor in their lives is this dual or multiple identity—they cease to be typical representatives of either, maintaining in their own person the diversity of their origins.

An opposite tendency in the contemporary world is towards larger homogenous groupings. Thus labels such as 'Western culture', 'Islamic culture', and 'South-East Asian culture' seem more viable than they once did. Perhaps there is even an emerging 'world culture'. There is evidence, for example, from very different languages and places, that service encounters increasingly follow a similar script. This is something along the lines of 'My name is x. How may I help you?' as a greeting, and 'Have a nice day' on parting. In an unpredictable world it would be foolish to forecast whether it is the forces for diversity or for homogeneity which will prove the stronger. In applied linguistics these complex influences and variations are factors which must be kept at the forefront of investigation.

Whatever our definition of culture, or our views about its universality, there can be little doubt that a real danger in the many activities which involve cross-cultural communication is misunderstanding. Consequently, in a wide range of personal and professional contexts, practical decisions must be made about how to avoid it.

Translation, culture, and context

Nowhere is this more apparent than in translation, where at every step decisions must be taken about when to provide explanation and extra detail, and how far to depart from the original. Even in the translation of a relatively simple business letter for example, there will be valid reasons not to use a literal translation but to mould what is said in one language to the conventions of another. 'Respected Gentleman Smith' may be the word-for-word translation of the Russian '*Uvazhayemy Gospodin Smith*', but 'Dear Mr Smith' is more appropriate in the context.

The study of translation—now commonly referred to as **translation studies**—has a far longer history than applied linguistics. Theories and practices of translation have changed but at their heart is a recurring debate, going back to classical times, about the degree to which a translator should attempt to render exactly what is said, or intervene to make the new text flow more smoothly, or achieve a similar effect as the original. This is by no means a simple matter. Word-for-word translation is impossible if the aim is to make sense. This is clear even when translating the most straightforward utterances between closely related languages. Take, for example, the French '*Ça me plaît*'.Translated word for word into English it is 'That me pleases'. At the very least, this demands reordering to 'That pleases me' to become a possible English sentence. Yet, in most circumstances, a more appropriate rendering would be 'I like it'. The issue therefore is not *whether* one should depart from the original but *how much*. Of necessity, translators and interpreters must make such judgements all the time.

These may seem to be linguistic rather than cultural matters. Indeed, they beg the question of the relationship between language and culture, for translation, as conventionally defined, is between languages not cultures. Yet, as even a simple example will show, translation cannot be conducted at a purely linguistic level but must incorporate cultural and contextual factors too. Take, for example, the translation of the English pronoun 'you' into a language which has a distinction between an informal second-person pronoun and a formal one (*tu* versus *vous* in French for example). In every instance a decision must be made about which to choose, and it cannot be based upon linguistic equivalence alone.

In many cases translation decisions can be a major factor in cross-cultural understanding and international affairs. The difficulties of translating news stories between Arabic and English provide many examples. Decisions have to be made about whether to gloss emotive words such as 'martyrdom', which has quite different connotations from the Arabic '*shahaada*', or simply to give up in difficult cases and import the original word, as in the case of 'jihad' and 'sharia', thus assuming in the reader a relevant background knowledge which they may not have. The importance of such decisions, playing as they do a role in each community's view of the other, cannot be underestimated.

'*Traduttore traditore*'—'The translator is a traitor'. This Italian adage provides its own illustration, for translated into English it loses the almost exact echo of the two words. It illustrates, too, why despite many attempts across the centuries, there can never be foolproof rules for doing a translation or precise ways of measuring its success. In every translation something must be lost. One cannot keep the sound *and* the word order *and* the exact nature of the phrase. One cannot always make, in Hymes' terms, the translation at once accurate, feasible, and appropriate. Yet translation is—in the (loosely translated!) words of Goethe—'impossible but necessary', essential both in world affairs and in individual lives. It is work at the boundaries of possibility, and when subjected to scrutiny it inevitably attracts criticism, like applied linguistics itself. There are always judgements and compromises to be made, reflecting the translator's evaluations both of the original text and of the translation's audience. This, incidentally, is why **machine translation** by computer, though it may provide a rough guide to what has been said, does not challenge the need for human judgement.

Own language: rights and understanding

The inevitable losses of translation lie behind the popular view that, if we are truly to understand someone and the culture from which they come, then it is necessary that we understand their language. This accounts for the widespread notion in literary and religious study that something essential is lost if texts cannot be read in the original. To a degree this view is motivated by some vague belief in 'the spirit of the language'; more precisely it derives from a belief that important ideas and traditions are specific to a particular language.

The corollary of this view is that if someone is to express themselves fully, they may need to do so in their own language. To preserve their culture, they must also have the right to educate their children in that language. These needs, which have been referred to as **language rights**, have clear implications for language planning. They are implicit in a good deal of national and international legislation, ensuring the possibility of own language use both in formal transactions and schools. On the other hand, there are many contexts where language rights are denied and linguistic majorities impose upon minorities, often through oppressive legislation. With increasing frequency such conditions contribute to languages dying out completely. In extensively multilingual and multicultural societies there are pressure groups seeking to preserve linguistic diversity and others seeking to restrict it. The 'English Only' movement in the USA is an example of the latter. Though the moral case for diversity seems self-evident, there are obvious practical problems in institutionalizing the use of every language, however small, in a community, and a valid practical need for at least one **lingua franca**. There is also the danger that language preservation, pursued in certain ways, can lead to segregation and sectarianism. The task of the language planner is to reconcile all of these interests and factors. Like that of the translator, it is inevitably thankless and controversial.

Teaching culture

Although relevant to every area of applied linguistics, the study of cross-cultural communication has often been related to ELT.

At first glance it seems sensible, when learning a language, also to study the culture of the people who speak it. While learning Icelandic—to return to the example used in Chapter 3—one would expect to study the lifestyle of the Icelanders. Thus, teaching materials could reasonably include an element of 'Icelandic studies' with descriptions of the treeless landscape, the historic links with Denmark, the importance of the fishing industry, and so on. For students such materials would be both necessary and motivating as they are unlikely to be studying the Icelandic language if they are not also interested in Icelandic culture.

With English however, and to a degree with other widely distributed languages such as Spanish and French, the situation is rather more complicated. Firstly, English is the language of many different cultures and the conventions governing its use vary accordingly. Our earlier example of 'How are you?' illustrates the point nicely. When used formulaically it functions differently in the USA, where it is a greeting on first introduction, and Britain, where it is a greeting on subsequent meetings. And when it is used as an actual enquiry about health or feelings it also elicits varying responses in different English-speaking communities.

Such variations, and the role of English as a global lingua franca, raise doubts about the association in many EFL materials of the English language with specific cultural practices, usually those of the dominant mainstream culture in either Britain or the USA. For some learners, whose need is to engage directly with one or other of these, such cultural bias may be valid, but for others, whose need is to use English outside such communities or who do not wish to absorb either British or American culture, the issue is considerably more complex. The question arises as to whether the cultural content of English as a lingua franca can be customized according to learner needs, or whether indeed the language needs to be associated with any culture at all. This, in turn, raises the larger issue of whether language and culture can be dissociated, and whether English can become the vehicle not only of specific local cultural identities but of 'world culture' as well. Can such a world culture be neutral or will it inevitably carry with it the values and beliefs of the societies whose language it has adopted?

These are issues resonant with ideological overtones, and individuals must make up their own minds about them. It is not for applied linguistics to do this for them. However what applied linguistics can do is to offer informed insights so that when decisions are made, as they necessarily must be in professional practice, both the facts and various interpretations of them are as clearly formulated as possible. The fraught area of intercultural communication is, in the modern world, at the very heart of applied linguistics.

Behind any applied linguistic discussion of culture is the difficult issue of the relation between a language and a culture and the degree to which one is implicated in the other. In linguistics the **linguistic relativity hypothesis**, which holds that language determines a unique way of seeing the world, has fallen from favour under the influence of Chomsky's emphasis on language as a biological rather than a social phenomenon. Yet, whatever the degree to which the language which we speak can determine our ways of thinking, it is certainly true that the linguistic choices we make *within* that language both reflect our ideology and influence the opinions of our audience. The ways in which linguistic choices construct values and meanings is particularly evident in the two areas of applied linguistics to which we turn our attention in Chapter 7.

7
Persuasion and poetics; rhetoric and resistance

'My father', begins the narrative of Jonathan Swift's *Gulliver's Travels*, 'had a small estate in Nottinghamshire; I was the third of five sons.' None of this is true: there never was a Captain Gulliver, and consequently no father or brothers. When Gulliver embarks upon his fantastic journeys the reader can be even more certain that there are no distant islands like Lilliput, populated with diminutive people. Yet we would never think of calling Swift a liar even though his language does not correspond to reality. We recognize the book as fiction. We enjoy it, lose ourselves in it, and indirectly learn from it some truths about the real world in which we *do* live—the one which is not created, as Gulliver's islands are, entirely by words.

Language, in literature, is used to create alternatives to the real world. In doing so, the precise choice and ordering of words is very important. It not only creates a surrogate world for us but also determines our attitude to its inhabitants and the events that take place there. Swift's opening sentence, for example, both gives us the details of Gulliver's family and origins and also indicates something of his character. His matter-of-fact tone and unembellished style suggest a blunt, no-nonsense kind of a fellow—one, therefore, to be trusted as he leads us through increasingly fantastic scenes.

This dependence upon precise wording is why a literary text loses so much in paraphrase or translation. Hamlet's 'To be, or not to be ...' is not exactly rendered either by the paraphrase 'Should I commit suicide ...', or the Spanish translation '*Ser o no ser* ...'. They change the resonance and rhythm of the original, and also differ in meaning.

Yet despite this importance of exact wording, the meanings of literary works are often disconcertingly inexact. They are notorious for their capacity to engender rival and often conflicting interpretations. And the greater the work, it seems, the greater the scope for disagreement. Was Hamlet mad or sane? Good or bad? Cruel or kind? Death force or life force? The play is endlessly interpreted and reinterpreted, on stage or in the mind, lending itself to the values and ideas of new generations, and different individuals and cultures.

What, though, does this have to do with applied linguistics? It is not, on the face of it, a practical problem of the sort we have been discussing so far. It does not have the same kind of direct social and economic consequences as language education policy, or the spread of English as a lingua franca. It would be wrong, however, to underestimate the impact and importance of literature. It reflects and constructs our individual and social identities; it embodies or criticizes the values of the society from which it comes; it has an essential role to play in education. And because it is constituted entirely of language, then analysis of that language must be relevant to our understanding of how it achieves such power. Such understanding—like applied linguistics—demands mediation between lived experience and academic knowledge.

Literary stylistics

Linguistic analysis, in other words, can describe and analyse the language of a literary text but is not of itself an *applied* linguistic activity. It begins to move in that direction, however, when linguistic choices are linked to their effects upon the reader and some attempt is made at an explanation. This is the endeavour of **literary stylistics**. It is not perhaps in itself applied linguistics as it involves no practical decision making, but it is, as we shall see, an important resource for the analysis of powerful and persuasive uses of language in general. It raises awareness, not only of the importance of exact wording but of how there is far more at stake in the use of language than the literal meaning of the words. Literary analysis, of its nature, cannot be brief if it is to do justice to its complex subject-matter and there is no space to go into any detail here. An example, however, can be found in the extract by Roger Fowler in Section 2.

Stylistic analyses tend to highlight three related aspects of literary language: its frequent deviation from the norms of more everyday language use; its patterning of linguistic units to create rhythms, rhymes, and parallel constructions; and the ways in which the form of the words chosen seems to augment or intensify the meaning. All these features are present in the melancholy opening stanza of William Blake's poem 'London'.

> I wander through each charter'd street
> Near where the charter'd Thames does flow
> And mark in every face I meet
> Marks of weakness, marks of woe.

Here we have repetitions of words ('charter'd', 'mark'); of sounds ('*w*eakness', '*w*oe'; '*m*ark', '*m*eet'); and of structures ('charter'd street', 'charter'd Thames'; 'Marks of weakness, marks of woe'). These establish a heavy tramping rhythm which reflects the sentiment and subject-matter of the poem. The word 'charter'd', moreover, is used in an innovative and idiosyncratic way, not to be precisely resolved by any dictionary definition and thus lending itself to many interpretations—'mapped' perhaps, or 'controlled by law'.

Such features of language use, frequently remarked upon in stylistics, are by no means exclusive to literature. They characterize other highly valued uses of language such as prayer, song, and rhetoric which, like literature, can comfort and strengthen, inspire and identify. More generally, if less nobly, they and other similar devices occur in persuasive and emotive uses of language in society at large, whether in commercial, political, or interpersonal communication. As with literature, stylistic analysis can investigate the link between the forms of these language uses and their social and psychological power. If such analysis is then used to address and uncover manipulation, and to empower those who are being manipulated, then it does indeed become part of an applied linguistic process.

Language and persuasion

Language can be used to tell the truth, whether it be literal truth or the more general truths of poetry or (for believers) prayer. Yet it can also be used to distort facts, or to persuade people to take a particular stance towards them. Literary language partakes of this persuasive power, but is perceived as inspiring and uplifting. It manipulates our feelings and thoughts though in ways which we are willing, even eager, to accept. Other uses of language are less benign, seeking to control and influence our ideas in the service of some vested political or commercial interest. Yet there is a sufficient degree of overlap for the techniques developed in the analysis of literary language to be extended to these other, more sinister, uses.

In its most straightforward form this dark side of language use is lying: the statement of untrue facts which, unlike literary fiction, are calculated to deceive us about the real world. Lies, however, once uncovered, are simply rejected. But there are other more subtle ways of using language to influence and mislead. In our contemporary 'information society', the need both to understand and to combat such language uses has become particularly pressing. We are assailed at every turn by carefully crafted words seeking to attract our attention, win our support, change our behaviour. Corporations, advertisers, politicians, journalists, pressure groups, scientists, celebrities—even shop assistants and telephone operators speaking from learned scripts—are busy telling us, not only what they and their organizations do, but also why it is good for us and for the world in general. And as global communication grows, so does the number of opposed and contradictory voices.

To make matters more complicated, it is very often impossible in many public discourses to pin down those responsible for what is said. There are many voices entangled in modern communication, each one, when questioned, passing on responsibility. Who is speaking, for example, in an advertisement? The corporation (and does that mean shareholders or management?), the agency (same question), the director, or the actors or models who appear in it? And which of these, if any, actually believes the claims which are made? Almost everyone is speaking for someone else. In assuming the persona of our job or organization, taking on the corporate voice, we become, in this respect, not only sinned against but sinning! This, too, is an area where techniques developed in literary analysis can be brought to bear. A multiplicity of voices is a feature of many literary works, especially novels and drama.

These are increasingly urgent issues, and applied linguistics should contribute to an understanding of them. This is not only because, as in the case of literary stylistics, the power of words is intrinsically interesting. It is rather that, both for individuals and for organizations, there are decisions to be made, often with far-reaching consequences for health, well-being, and prosperity. These decisions will depend in part upon the capacity to see through the way language is being used to the facts and intentions which it realizes. How should we interpret what we read in the mission statement, the 'scientific' report, or the food label? To what degree should we believe what we hear on the news, or from our politicians' mouths? Which side should we take when there are disagreements, over the effects of new technology on health and the environment for example, or the rival claims of two sides in a military conflict? Understanding linguistic techniques of persuasion can enhance our ability to make the rational informed judgements on which decision making depends. It is here that applied linguistics has a particular contribution to make, and here that some of the skills developed in literary stylistics can be extended to very powerful effect.

Critical Discourse Analysis (CDA)

There is, of course, in any communication an inevitable selection and omission of information. Newspaper editors must choose which events to cover, how much space to devote to each, and which facts to emphasize or omit. Thus a tabloid paper might decide to cover a celebrity divorce as a front page story while a broadsheet might give more space to an economic forecast, omitting the celebrity divorce or mentioning it only in the briefest possible terms. It is not that the process of selection and omission is wrong in itself. One cannot report any event or situation, however truthfully, without selecting some facts in preference to others. But the selection, equally inevitably, reflects the values of the writer and the view of the world which he or she wishes to encourage in their reader.

These matters, however, are already apparent to the perceptive reader with or without any specialized knowledge of language. Of more interest to applied linguists, and of more danger for being less transparent, is the presentation of the same facts in ways which, while not altering the truth of what is said, nevertheless influence, and are perhaps calculated to influence, the reader's attitude. Thus just as a glass might be described as 'half full' or 'half empty' with rather different implications, so the same food item can be truthfully described as either '90% fat-free' or '10% fat'. Both are equally true, but to a consumer bent upon reducing their calorie intake the former description seems more attractive. As in a literary text, the wording is all. 'What's done is done' says the confident Lady Macbeth after the play's opening scenes; 'What's done cannot be undone' is her remorseful lament at the end. The literal meaning is the same, but the effect is very different. It is in precise analysis of such detail that a real contribution can be made to people's capacity to read and listen critically, and to resist being manipulated by what is said. The analysis of such language and its effects is known as **critical linguistics**, or, when placed in a larger social context and seen as part of a process of social change, as **Critical Discourse Analysis (CDA)**.

One area of interest is the many ways in which language merges opinion with fact. The most obvious is apparently descriptive vocabulary which incorporates a judgement, for example, 'regime' for 'government', 'terrorist' for 'combatant', 'murder' for 'killing'. The point here is not that the judgement itself is necessarily wrong but that there is no separation of fact and opinion. More subtle choices of vocabulary include reference to some countries by name and others by their inhabitants, for example, 'Spain has complained to the Russians' in a BBC news headline, or the introduction of 'we' and 'our' to mean 'the people of this country', with the alarming implication that the news is for insiders only. Grammatical devices, as well as vocabulary, can achieve similar effects. 'Fears are rising that ...' fails to say who is afraid, suggesting this is how the news writer thinks people ought to feel rather than how they actually do feel. 'The President threatened to suppress opposition' interprets the

President's words for us rather than, by quoting them, allowing us to make our own judgement.

A further area of interest, less evident without linguistic analysis, is persistent patterns of grammatical choice. There are, for example, constructions which allow a speaker or writer not to mention the agent (i.e. the person responsible for something). Two strategies in particular allow this to happen. One is **passivization**, the favouring of passive constructions over active ones, for example, 'Five children were killed in the air attack' not 'The pilots killed five children'. The other is **nominalization**, when actions and processes are referred to by nouns as though they, rather than the people doing them, were the agent, for example, 'Genetic modification is a powerful technique' rather than 'Researchers who modify genes have a great deal of power'. Both nominalization and passivization can make an action seem both inevitable and impersonal, for example, 'Redundancies will be announced' rather than 'The owners will be firing people'.

It is by no means only in overtly political matters that the techniques of CDA can be brought to bear. An area increasingly affecting all our lives is the communication of new scientific research and its technological applications in areas such as medicine, food production, and information technology. Non-specialists legitimately wish to make informed decisions about the impact of this research on individual lives, social developments, and the environment. They are also aware of vested commercial and political interests in particular lines of research, and a consequent blurring of the traditional lines between objective scientific and commercial persuasive discourse. Science has become political. In this situation there is a pressing need to develop awareness of how language is used in the presentation of technical information. This is an applied linguistic issue in which CDA has a particularly important role to play.

This situation is part of a larger phenomenon in which specialists whose work is of great social importance are confronted with the need to communicate their specialized knowledge to the outside world. There is a tendency, when doing this, to move in two opposite directions: one towards obfuscation and the other towards a false clarity.

Obfuscation is the failure to speak as plainly and straight-forwardly as possible. In addition to the language of applied science, that of the law and bureaucracy are often cited as examples. In their defence, it is often argued that clarity should be sacrificed to exactitude. The scientist must be true to the facts; the lawyer must foresee every possible loophole. On the other hand, it may be that language is being used as a screen and its obscurity functioning to guard the specialists' territories and vested interests from democratic scrutiny. In these cases, what the critical discourse analyst must do is investigate whether in a particular instance there would be loss if more straightforward language were used. Similar arguments pertain to all specialized professional discourse. It is exceedingly difficult in this area to distinguish necessary complexity of expression from unnecessary disguise of information and the use of specialized language to overawe and intimidate.

The other tendency has been described by the critical discourse analyst Norman Fairclough as **conversationalization** and the creation of **synthetic personality**. This is the tendency for communication, however complex or significant or however unequal the encounter, to be presented in the register of casual conversation, as though the relationship between the participants were equal and intimate. This presents the opposite danger from obfuscation, for it may make matters simple and imprecise which need more attention. It also fails to mark in any way those areas of human intercourse, such as the law and scientific enquiry, which legitimately demand both indicators of their power and greater attention to detail.

There is, however, a potential problem with CDA analyses which has been noted by several applied linguists. This is that they risk attributing too much intentionality to the writer and too much passivity to the reader. Most texts are both constructed and interpreted in many different ways. Although there may be cases where choices are made deliberately, the process of composition is often likely to be a more hasty and *ad hoc* affair, determined by conventions and many other factors. Readings, too, are diverse. Some are well-informed and careful, already aware of bias; others are casual, unlikely to be swayed by one precise choice of words or another. There is, in short, a danger of assuming that interpretation of a text is wholly determined by the language used.

These are difficult matters, but they are areas of language use which affect everyone, and it is impossible to underestimate their potential effect upon our individual lives. In a competitive and dangerous world, being able to understand and to assess the information we receive and the motives and interests of those who are giving it to us is of essential importance. This is part of knowing a language and one on which—quite literally—our futures depend. Inevitably, there are pitfalls in CDA as there must be in any enterprise which touches upon, and seeks to intervene in, matters of great personal and social significance. It may end up presuming to speak for people rather than informing the way in which they speak for themselves, and it may develop an obfuscatory jargon of its own. As in other controversial and sensitive areas of enquiry the applied linguist, when drawing upon CDA, must struggle to achieve a delicate balance. But the alternative is not to engage at all, which undermines the rationale for applied linguistics as a whole. Dealing with and understanding the persuasive and manipulative use of language is a major need in the contemporary world. Being able to do this effectively is essential to us all.

8
Past, present, and future directions

The purpose of this final chapter is to review the past and current state of applied linguistics, assessing both present and potential developments. In doing so, it revisits the themes of Chapter 1 in the light of the intervening exploration.

Early orientation

A great deal has been written about the origin of the term 'applied linguistics' and inevitably there is some disagreement as to where and when it was first used. What is agreed, however, is that it emerged in tandem with, and in response to, the changing international linguistic landscape after World War II. The term rapidly gained currency, importance, and followers from the late 1950s and into the 1960s, and has thrived ever since.

At first its concerns were almost exclusively with TEFL. In its early days, the nature of the subject seemed relatively straightforward. It might be caricatured as follows: linguists knew about language; applied linguists made this knowledge available to English language teachers; the consequence was that language learning was improved. The direction of influence, in other words, was seen as one-way and unproblematic. This transmissive approach has been described, critically, by the applied linguist Henry Widdowson, as 'linguistics applied'.

Subsequent changes

Since the early days, a good deal has changed in both the content and theoretical underpinning of the subject. Firstly, there is the issue of scope. Although there are still many publications and courses which equate the field with TEFL, this narrow remit is generally giving way to a much broader one encompassing many other areas of enquiry, as outlined in Chapter 1.

Secondly, there is the relationship with linguistics. Many contemporary applied linguists are less willing to regard linguistics as their 'parent discipline' than their predecessors. They feel that the engagement with practice has given the subject a distinctive identity, and that applied linguistics has its own theories which contribute to, rather than merely derive from, linguistics. They see applied linguistics, in other words, as an autonomous discipline in its own right. There are also those who would take this further and see the boundary between linguistics and applied linguistics dissolved in favour of a single discipline. They argue that the current Chomskyan focus upon the biological and cognitive aspects of language fundamentally distorts its nature, and prefer to see language as intrinsically social, inseparable from the kinds of issue we have discussed in this book.

Yet another source of change has been new attitudes and ideas among professionals, especially teachers. In recent years there have been many critiques of the earlier relationship between professional practice and academic knowledge, indicating a greater reluctance to accept handed-down knowledge without question. Thus, just as applied linguistics has asserted its independence from linguistics, even sometimes seeking to rewrite the linguistics agenda, so language-teaching professionals have also asserted their right to approach applied linguistics selectively and warily, making their own decisions about what is relevant and how it is best applied.

There are, then, tensions at all interfaces of the old three-way relationship between linguists, applied linguists, and language professionals. Changes, inevitably, have led to some division and disagreement. However this is by no means something to be deplored. Applied linguistics may be less stable and more prone to factional argument than in the past but it is also more dynamic and more exciting.

Second-Language Acquisition (SLA)

Differing views do not always, however, lead to confrontation and debate. They may also lead to separate development. The field has undergone a degree of fragmentation in which different areas of enquiry, while still under the auspices of applied linguistics, have developed their own fairly autonomous research communities. One highly active area of enquiry of this kind has been the field of **Second-Language Acquisition (SLA)** research.

From the 1960s onwards, great strides were made in first-language acquisition research. Taking its cue from these, and starting in earnest in the 1970s, SLA research concerned itself with both explaining and describing the process of acquiring a second language. (In this context, 'second language' is used to refer to any additional language, embracing both foreign languages and second languages in the more limited sense.) It has looked at the route, the rate, and the end state of SLA, and the ways in which it is affected by external factors such as instruction, interaction, and motivation. Particular areas of interest have included the degree of transfer from the first language/s, the degree of systematicity in learners' language, variation between learners or within one learner, and—most of all perhaps—why the process of acquiring a second language, as opposed to acquiring a first language, is so often regarded as 'incomplete'. Lastly, the findings of SLA research have frequently been drawn upon to suggest ways of improving language teaching and learning.

Undoubtedly a great deal has been discovered by SLA research, and many interesting explanations advanced. Yet valid reservations have also been expressed, both about the research itself and about attempts to relate it to language teaching (reservations which, interestingly, are shared by Chomsky). All of these touch upon matters of concern which we have encountered in earlier chapters. One point of criticism is the frequent assumption—betrayed by generic use of the term '*the* learner'—of a universalist model of the kind developed for first language acquisition in Chomskyan linguistics. In this, the process of SLA is considered to be more or less the same for all learners, relatively unaffected either by external variables or by differences between languages. However appropriate this model may be for first language acquisition, where there are elements common to the experience of every child, for SLA it is much less convincing. In second language learning there are manifest differences between learners and learning contexts, with consequent differences of outcome. Another point of criticism, betrayed by the very term *second* language acquisition, is the frequent implication that monolingualism is the normal starting point for language learners. Very little account has been taken in SLA of learners who are adding a language to an existing repertoire of more than one. 'Additional language acquisition' would be a much more appropriate term.

More fundamental still are doubts which have been expressed about the possibility of SLA research being conducted, as it often purports to be, in a scientific manner. Here, the argument is that, given the extent of individual and sociological variables, the difficulties of replicating the same learning situation, and the subjective nature of measuring success, conclusions cannot be as factual and reliable as we are led to believe. In addition it is said that even if claims and findings are reliable and generalizable, there remains a need to adjust them to differing educational and cultural traditions. Mediation, in other words, is needed between the knowledge of 'the experts' and the wishes and wants of individual students and teachers. The latter, too, have their own valid ideas about how language learning is best conducted and it is unlikely that the process will be successful if these are not taken into account. The classic example of this is the resistance by many teachers and learners to SLA claims in the 1980s that language acquisition can take place without explicit learning of rules, translation, and grading of structures.

In recent years, such criticisms have been voiced with increasing frequency and persuasiveness. They do not, however, apply to all SLA research, but only to what may be described as its mainstream. There are also richer and more context-sensitive approaches now gathering momentum. They recognize the diverse and imprecise nature of SLA, allowing the findings of research to be made relevant to widely varying types of educational situation.

Corpus linguistics

Another area of enquiry which is currently very active, also often associated with applied linguistics, is **corpus linguistics**. The word 'corpus' (plural 'corpora') refers to a databank of language which has actually occurred—whether written, spoken, or a mixture of the two. Corpus linguistics is concerned with the patterns and regularities of language use which can be revealed by systematic analysis of such corpora. Before computers, some headway was made in this kind of study by collecting printed corpora, laboriously reading through them, and manually recording facts. In recent years, however, corpus linguistics has been transformed by electronic storage and automatic searching. Millions of words can be searched within seconds to yield extensive information about word frequencies and word combinations. This is why corpus linguistics has made such extraordinary advances in the last few decades. The results have been staggering, not only because of the descriptive facts uncovered but also because of their implications for linguistic theory and for our understanding of what it means to learn and know a language.

One of the most important insights relates to **collocations**, i.e. frequent combinations of words. A far greater proportion of language use is composed of collocations than was previously imagined. There are countless combinations of words which are grammatically possible but do not occur, or occur only rarely, but there are collocations with very similar meanings which occur with great frequency. It is much more usual, for example, to say 'provide assistance' than 'supply assistance', even though both are possible. In this and many other ways corpus linguistics provides us with information about the previously neglected fourth parameter of Hymes' communicative competence, attestedness (i.e. what is actually done), discussed in Chapter 5.

As records of language behaviour, corpora cannot tell us directly how language is represented in the mind. The fact that something occurs frequently in a corpus does not necessarily mean that it is processed as a ready-made unit by each individual user. Nevertheless, the prominence of collocation does strongly suggest a greater role for memory in language processing than was previously thought. Language processing may be less a question of slotting individual words into a grammatical structure and far more a question of deploying larger units made up of several words.

In recent years, many writers have argued strongly that corpus findings should fundamentally alter the way in which we teach languages. If native-like use of language depends largely upon remembering ready-made units, then, they argue, it seems sensible to shift attention away from grammar towards vocabulary, or even to rethink the validity of the traditional distinction between the two. Knowing a word entails knowing the grammatical constructions into which it often fits; knowing a grammatical structure involves knowing the words which are likely to realize it.

Yet the applications of corpus linguistics are far wider than language teaching. It has revolutionized lexicography, allowing dictionary writers to provide much more information about the use and context of words, and more representative examples. It can be used to establish the authorship of a document by analysing an individual's style, providing forensic linguists and literary scholars with crucial evidence about whether or not a document is a fake. In CDA it can show whether certain grammatical or lexical choices regularly occur in relation to certain topics. The number of potential applications is open-ended, and immense.

Being applied

SLA and corpus linguistics have different approaches to language and are concerned with different areas of enquiry. SLA is predominantly psychological in orientation, focused upon how a language develops in the mind. Corpus linguistics, on the other hand, is predominantly social, studying the language behaviour of people who are already proficient in language use. Yet, in their relationship to applied linguistics, they also have a certain amount in common. Both lay claim to having uncovered objective scientific facts about language—SLA about learning, corpus linguistics about use—and both, at times, assume that such findings should be the main factor in language-related decision making.

Yet while many findings of both have a great deal of relevance to decision making, this is not automatically the case. Relevance may need, rather, to be achieved through integration with other perspectives, and the approach to language reshaped in the context of the problem which is being addressed. It is questionable, in other words, whether either SLA or corpus linguistics can be, of itself, *applied* linguistics.

Take, for example, the discussion in Chapter 3 about models of English for language education and the degree to which one of the standard native Englishes should continue to be the goal of all learners. As we have seen, the solution to this problem is by no means straightforward. The stance which is taken on it cannot be, of its nature, entirely dispassionate and scientific. It must also be in part evaluative and political. Factual information such as word frequencies in native English cannot therefore be the determining factors in the kind of English which learners want or need to learn.

Or take the issues surrounding formal versus 'natural' foreign language learning. Even if it could be shown by SLA that additional languages can be largely acquired without instruction, that may not, as we have seen, fit with learner or teacher wishes, or with educational traditions. Decisions about language teaching inevitably involve judgements about what it means to know and use the language correctly, and about desirable educational practice. They also need to be tailored to particular contexts. There is a danger, if such factors are not taken into account, that 'scientific approaches', used too prescriptively, become new versions of Widdowson's 'linguistics applied'.

Critical Applied Linguistics (CALx)

Throughout the earlier chapters of this book we have seen that academic research alone cannot fully elucidate the most urgent applied linguistic issues. Inevitably, decision making also involves both political evaluation and moral judgement. This realization is among the factors which have contributed to some recent arguments for a radical new departure.

In **Critical Applied Linguistics (CALx)**, applied linguistics abandons its apparently neutral stance and aligns itself more explicitly with political action. It becomes intrinsically 'critical' in the sense of being politically committed and challenging. The proponents of CALx argue that the discipline does not cease to be rational or factual; on the contrary, it becomes more rational by acknowledging the inevitable. Among the main principles proposed for the new approach are that it should be engaged with social change and action, and combat injustice and inequality. In this cause, it should incorporate work in critical political theory into applied linguistics, constantly relating the micro domain of language use in interpersonal settings to the macro domain of broader social, cultural, and political struggles. Lastly, it should be self-critical, constantly questioning and reassessing itself.

This approach seems persuasive, if only because, as we have seen, political and applied linguistics issues cannot be divorced. Active involvement in decision making about language is part of the very definition of applied linguistics, and whether at the micro or macro level, such action must necessarily involve both evaluation and political judgement. Nevertheless valid criticisms of CALx have been expressed, and not necessarily, as proponents of CALx would like us to believe, from a right-wing or reactionary standpoint. Firstly, it can be pointed out that CALx's claims to political commitment are extremely vague. It is not clear exactly what political action it proposes or what kind of political system it seeks to promote. To claim that one should be 'opposed to injustice' is something with which everyone, of all political persuasions, would agree. The problem comes with specific instances. Was US bombing of Afghanistan justified? Should fishing jobs be cut to save fish stocks? Should health services be run only by the state? Such specific questions are seldom answered in CALx. It can be argued that in addition, rather than promoting those vague causes which it does espouse, CALx may have the opposite effect because people are more likely to change their mind as the result of a factual reasoned argument than one based on assertion. Lastly, and perhaps most damningly, it is not really clear what is new about CALx other than the word 'critical'. Linguists and applied linguists have long used their research to combat injustices, both on a micro and a macro level, without needing this epithet: for example, in the fields of social and ethnic discrimination, language death, prejudice against deaf sign languages, and the use of fabricated evidence in criminal trials.

'Post-modern' applied linguistics

Like SLA and corpus linguistics, CALx starts with a 'grand narrative', both about the abstractions of linguistics and about the experience of language which dominates all our lives, and interprets everything in its light. In the case of CALx this narrative is a political credo rather than an objective scientific research paradigm. But the direction is the same. The starting point is a set of abstract and idealized facts, and the movement is from them to the actual problem about which a decision needs to be made. If you like, instead of 'linguistics applied' we have 'politics applied'.

A very different kind of approach, often confused with CALx (even by its proponents!) is one which, in the spirit of post-modernism, abandons 'grand narratives' altogether and relocates the impetus for action within the problem itself. In this view, those with language related problems should seek relevant advice in a practical and expedient manner. Thus, while they might turn to linguistics, they might also equally well seek advice from other academic disciplines, singly or in combination, or indeed outside the academic field altogether. In this view, applied linguistics should not be an autonomous discipline seeking to formulate, independently, principles of general applicability and relevance. It should become instead a responsive discipline, assembled occasionally as it were, for a specific purpose. The worth of research and theorizing, if they were needed at all, would be measured in terms of their usefulness. Such an approach reverses the direction of influence so that it no longer flows from the academic linguistics through applied linguistics to practitioners, but the other way.

While there are a number of apparent attractions to such an approach—it can be seen, for example, as a way of empowering teachers and other language professionals—there are also a number of dangers and less attractive elements too. Most obviously there is the danger to intellectual enquiry posed by any activity which is driven by purely practical criteria. If something is not seen as useful and profitable in the short term, then it is not worth thinking about. In addition, there is the obvious point that this approach may be exploited by employers, corporations, and governments, whose interest is neither in language professionals nor in people at the receiving end of language policies, but in various self-seeking agendas of their own.

A harder future: mediation

Applied linguistics is concerned with the most emotive and most important issues: the education of children, the rights of the disadvantaged, the changing balance of cultures and languages, the effects of technology on communication. These are global issues, but they are manifested in personal decision making too. As such, under pressure from all sides, it is faced with a number of options. Some are easy, but ultimately unsatisfactory. One is harder, but rewarding, both for society at large, and for applied linguists themselves.

Being as it is at the interface between academic enquiry and professional practice, one easy option is to follow the instructions of either one or the other, so that applied linguistics becomes simply the messenger of academic researchers or the servant of professional expediency. Another easy option is to become a vaguely formulated political campaign, though one more focused upon its own credentials than upon the redress of any particular injustices. Yet another is to indulge in a disappearing act, appealing to the slippery concept of **interdisciplinarity**, as though applied linguistics existed only at the intersection of other fields, or were an *ad hoc* assemblage.

There are many voices speaking to applied linguistics—too many to do justice to in a short introduction such as this. Applied linguistics must listen to them all. But it must not then simply repeat what it has heard, allowing the loudest and most powerful voices to drown out the others. If it is to fulfil its aspirations, if it is to have any worth in its own right, if it is to be listened to, and if it is to intervene successfully in the many urgent language related problems of the modern world, then it must also have a voice of its own. This will not be the same as any one of its parts, nor even the mechanical assembly of them all. It will be rather an emergent, autonomous, dynamic, exciting, and influential voice—one which can speak authoritatively, to and about the abstract formulations and findings of linguistics, and the experience of language use which dominates all of our lives.

Readings

Chapter 1
Applied linguistics

Text 1
H.G.WIDDOWSON: 'Models and Fictions' in
H.G. Widdowson: *Explorations in Applied Linguistics 2.*
Oxford University Press 1984, pages 21–2, 27

*The seminal paper from which this text is taken changed the
nature and direction of applied linguistics. In it the author
argues that the function of applied linguistics should not
merely be to transmit findings from linguistics to those
involved with language related problems. It should rather be
to mediate between linguistic theory and professional
practice, making each relevant to the other.*

Our activity has commonly been called *applied linguistics*. A
metathetic alternative has been suggested: *linguistics applied*.
What do we understand by these two terms and which of them
provides the most appropriate designation for what we do?

I assume that, semantically, the difference between the two
expressions is that in the case of *applied linguistics* we have a
type classification, ... whereas with *linguistics applied* we do not.
We might compare *Lost paradise* with *Paradise lost*. On the one
hand a type of paradise, a palm-fringed beach perhaps, thronged
with lotus eaters; on the other hand, the fall of man, the unique
loss of Eden. Thus applied linguistics can be understood as a kind
of linguistics, like historical linguistics or folk linguistics. This
presumably allows its practitioners to define an independent per-

spective on the general phenomena of language and to establish principles of enquiry without necessary reference to those which inform linguistics *tout court* and *tel quel*. With linguistics applied we do not have this option. Whatever we do with linguistics, however we apply it, the informing principles which define this area of enquiry, already pre-established, must remain intact. Any other principles we invoke must be auxiliary operating principles and have to do not with theory as such but with the technology of application.

It seems to me, then, that with linguistics applied the theory of language and the models of description deriving from it must be those of linguistics. As an activity, therefore, it is essentially conformist. Applied linguistics, on the other hand, can develop its own non-conformist theory, its own relevant models of description. Both lines of approach have their dangers. The tendency of linguistics applied will be to dance attendance to whatever tune is currently in theoretical fashion. The tendency of applied linguistics will be to dance around in circles with no tune at all. For linguistics applied, therefore, the question of central concern is: how far can existing models of description in linguistics be used to resolve the practical problems of language use we are concerned with? For applied linguistics, the central question is: how can *relevant* models of language description be devised, and what are the factors which will determine their effectiveness?...

My own belief is that it is only by preferring applied linguistics to linguistics applied that we shall achieve something which is relevant and accountable in terms of usefulness and avoid the kind of ethnocentrism and cultural imposition that has marked so much of language study and teaching in the past. There are signs of this preference emerging in recent work. But we have a long way to go and there will be many an alluring linguistic Will-o'-the-wisp to lead us astray from the path of our intentions.

▷ *What does Widdowson mean by the remark that 'the tendency of applied linguistics will be to dance around in circles with no tune at all'? What kind of tune is he proposing to remedy this tendency?*

▷ *In the last sentence, Widdowson refers to 'many an alluring linguistic Will-o'-the-wisp to lead us astray'. What kind of thing does he have in mind? What examples have you encountered while reading this book?*

———

Texts 2, 3, and 4 are intended to illustrate the range of applied linguistic research and practice. They concern three areas which, for reasons of space, have not been described in detail in this book: forensic linguistics, translating and interpreting, and clinical linguistics.

Text 2

MALCOLM COULTHARD: 'The official version: audience manipulation in police records of interviews with suspects' in C.R. Caldas-Coulthard and M. Coulthard (eds.): *Texts and Practices*. Routledge 1996, pages 166–8

In this extract, the author introduces some of the ways in which linguistic analysis can provide important evidence in criminal proceedings. The chapter from which it is taken goes on to describe in detail how the author, using insights from discourse analysis, was able to demonstrate that a police record of an interview had been altered after the event.

In the English, Welsh, and Northern Irish Courts, though not the Scottish, an unsigned confession is sufficient to convict, even if its authenticity is disputed and there is no other supporting forensic evidence. Thus the accuracy of the record of what an accused (is claimed to have) said while in custody can assume tremendous importance. Ideally the Court is presented with a complete verbatim record of what was said ... and then it makes its own decision about the meaning and behavioural consequences of the crucial utterance(s), that is, their *illocutionary and perlocutionary forces*. However, for a whole series of reasons, the situation is rarely ideal.

Perhaps the most famous example of a problematic situation, the case of Derek Bentley and Chris Craig, dates from the 1950s. The two young men were apprehended by police as they were trying to break into a warehouse. Bentley, already under arrest at the time, was said to have shouted to Craig, who had a revolver, 'Let him have it, Chris'; shortly afterwards Craig fired several shots and killed a policeman. The debate in court over the interpretation of the ambiguous utterance was resolved in favour of the incriminating performative, 'I hereby urge you to shoot him', the perlocutionary effect of which, the death of a policeman, made Bentley an accessory to murder, for which he was convicted and subsequently hanged.

In his defence Bentley did not deny the Court's interpretation but rather, more radically, the fact that he had uttered the phrase at all: he asserted that it was a complete invention of the police officers involved in his arrest. Bentley's claim, that linguistic evidence had been in part or even totally invented by the police, was to be reiterated by many others down the years, although claims by the convicted that they had been 'verballed' were usually viewed with great scepticism by the general public—at least until 1989. This consensus began to change, however, following the case of one Paul Dandy, where it was irrefutably demonstrated, by means of Electro-Static Deposition Analysis (ESDA)—a technique which allows the analyst to read impressions and indentations which have been created on the particular sheet being examined by the pressure of the instrument used to write on the sheet above ... that the final page of an otherwise authentic interview record had been rewritten to allow the insertion of ... two incriminating utterances ...

As a result of the disquiet created by such cases the police system for recording interviews with an accused has changed significantly, at least in England—now a significant proportion of interviews are video-recorded and almost all of the rest are audio-taped using stereo tapes with a voice announcing the time at 10-second intervals already pre-recorded on to one track, in order to prevent subsequent editing, deletion of expletives, and so on.

In this chapter, however, I do not propose to focus on cases of purported invented and incriminating evidence, but rather on more subtle examples where what was recorded and the ways in which it was recorded have introduced bias that could have affected the judge and jury's general impression of the character of the police officers and the accused. In so doing this bias created a frame within which other utterances which *were* incriminating were interpreted.

▷ At the end of this text, Coulthard says that he will be moving on to 'more subtle examples' than the Bentley case. Does that imply that the resolution of the Bentley case, and other similar ones, does not demand any linguistic expertise, but merely 'common sense'?

▷ Consider this text in the light of Text 1's distinction between 'linguistics applied' and 'applied linguistics'. Which is this an instance of, and why?

Text 3

MONA BAKER: *In Other Words: A Coursebook on Translation.*
Routledge 1992, pages 4–5

In this text, Baker argues for the importance of a knowledge of contemporary linguistics for professional translators.

Most translators prefer to think of their work as a profession and would like to see others treat them as professionals rather than as skilled or semi-skilled workers. But to achieve this, translators need to develop an ability to stand back and reflect on what they do and how they do it. Like doctors and engineers, they have to prove to themselves as well as others that they are in control of what they do; that they do not just translate well because they have a 'flair' for translation, but rather because, like other professionals, they have made a conscious effort to understand various aspects of their work.

Unlike medicine and engineering, translation is a very young discipline in academic terms. It is only just starting to feature as a subject of study in its own right, not yet in all but in an increasing number of universities and colleges around the world. Like any young discipline, it needs to draw on the findings and theories of other related disciplines in order to develop and formalize its own methods; but which disciplines it can naturally and fruitfully be related to is still a matter of some controversy. Almost every aspect of life in general and of the interaction between speech communities in particular can be considered relevant to translation, a discipline which has to concern itself with how meaning is generated within and between various groups of people in various cultural settings. This is clearly too big an area to investigate in one go. So, let us just start by saying that, if translation is ever to become a profession in the full sense of the word, translators will need something other than the current mixture of intuition and practice to enable them to reflect on what they do and how they do it. They will need, above all, to acquire a sound knowledge of the raw material with which they work: to understand what language is and how it comes to function for its users.

Linguistics is a discipline which studies language both in its own right and as a tool for generating meanings. It should therefore have a great deal to offer to the budding discipline of translation studies; it can certainly offer translators valuable insights into the nature and function of language. This is particularly true of modern linguistics, which no longer restricts itself to the study of language *per se* but embraces such sub-disciplines as textlinguistics (the study of text as a communicative event rather than as a shapeless string of words and structures) and pragmatics (the study of language in use rather than language as an abstract system). This book attempts to explore some areas in which modern linguistic theory can provide a basis for training translators and can inform and guide the decisions they have to make in the course of performing their work.

▷ *What are Baker's main reasons for advocating the study of linguistics by trainee translators? Is it simply usefulness, or something more besides?*

▷ *As with Text 2, consider this text in the light of Text 1's distinction between 'linguistics applied' and 'applied linguistics'. Which is this an instance of, and why?*

Text 4

MICHAEL PERKINS and SARA HOWARD: 'Principles of clinical linguistics' and JULIE MORRIS and SUE FRANKLIN: 'Aphasia: assessment and remediation of a speech discrimination deficit' in Michael Perkins and Sara Howard (eds.): *Case Studies in Clinical Linguistics*. Whurr Publishers 1995, pages 11–12, 245–6

This text draws together extracts from two different parts of the book. In the first extract, Michael Perkins and Sara Howard discuss the relation of theory and practice in clinical linguistics. The second extract, from a chapter by Julie Morris and Sue Franklin, gives details of a patient suffering from aphasia and indicates the kind of practical situation with which speech therapists are confronted.

Any clinical linguistic analysis or therapy programme presupposes some theoretical basis no matter how impoverished and unacknowledged, and any insightful analysis of clinical data will invariably raise issues that have potential theoretical implications for language in general. ...

Unfortunately for practitioners such as speech and language therapists, however, theoretical models of language inevitably involve a high degree of abstractness. Generative linguistic theory, for example, attempts to represent our underlying knowledge of language, but the extent to which such representations have psychological validity and relate to language use is far from clear. Cognitive-neuropsychological models ... have the advantage of representing psychological processes underlying language use rather than mere knowledge of language, but even here the relationship between the modelled representation and the purported process itself remains unclear.

Although theorists and practitioners may be interested in the same phenomena, their aims are quite different. Theorists are only ultimately interested in clinical linguistic behaviour to the extent that it may confirm or disconfirm their hypotheses about the nature of language. Speech and language therapists, on the other hand, are only interested in linguistic theory—at least in their remedial role—to the extent that it may be of some clinical use. Nevertheless, the theoretical needs of speech and language therapists are very real. Theory is needed to provide answers to questions such as:

– How is language organized and represented in the brain?
– How is language produced and understood?
– How does a given instance of abnormal language differ from a target norm?
– In cases of language loss, what has been lost, and therefore what needs to be replaced?
– In cases of developmental disorder, what forms and functions still need to be acquired, and in what order?

The fact that current linguistic theory can provide only partial and provisional answers does not render the questions any less crucial.

———

JS presented with difficulties understanding spoken language. This was particularly marked if the topic of conversation was rapidly changed or if the subject of conversation was not obvious. JS's responses to questions often showed some vague awareness of the topic of conversation. He reported difficulties with newspaper reading, although he continued to enjoy looking at his daily paper. Functionally JS's own communication was good. JS used single words and short phrases combined with gesture, facial expression and reliance on context to express his message. He was also adept at using the listener to ask him questions about his intended message, and informed them if they had misinterpreted his attempt. Communication with people other than family members was usually restricted to social greetings etc., which JS had no difficulty with. It will be JS's problems with spoken word comprehension that are the main focus of the discussion here.

▷ As in Text 3, the first extract here discusses the relation between theory and professional practice, arguing that practitioners (in this case speech therapists) need knowledge of linguistic theory. To what extent are the reasons given similar to those advanced in Text 3 for translators?

▷ Consider the case details in the second extract. What factors other than linguistic theory will be relevant to therapy for this patient?

▷ As with Texts 2 and 3, consider this text in the light of Text 1's distinction between 'linguistics applied' and 'applied linguistics'. Which is this an instance of, and why?

Chapter 2
Prescribing and describing: popular and academic views of 'correctness'

Text 5
DEBORAH CAMERON: *Verbal Hygiene*. Routledge 1995, pages 3–4

In this text, Deborah Cameron takes issue with descriptivism in linguistics on the grounds that: a) it divorces language from the experience of its users b) it is itself a type of prescriptivism.

Prescriptivism is negative for linguists in two senses. First, it is negative in the everyday sense of being a bad or wrong thing. The typical attitude to it among linguists runs the gamut from despair at prescribers' ignorance to outrage at their bigotry, and is aptly if apocalyptically summed up in the title of a 1950 book by Robert Hall, *Leave Your Language Alone*. Apart from its sternly negative tone, which is obvious enough, this title also implies a separation of language from its users: rather like those shop assistants and bank clerks who complain that if only the customers would stop bothering them they would be able to get on with some work, the phrase 'leave your language alone' suggests that language would be better off without the constant unwelcome attentions of its speakers.

This is an attitude that I would want to question. When I suggested earlier that making value judgements on language is an integral part of using it and not an alien practice 'perversely grafted on', I was implicitly taking issue with the assumptions made in this finger-wagging tradition, where the evaluative concerns of speakers (embodied in their 'prescriptivism') are by implication seen as both alien and perverse.

One important point to make about the anti-prescriptivist 'leave your language alone' tradition within linguistics is that in a certain sense it mirrors the very same value-laden attitudes it seems to be criticizing. All attitudes to language and linguistic change are fundamentally ideological, and the relationship between popular and expert ideologies, though it is complex and conflictual, is closer than one might think.

▷ In Chapter 2, we pursued the notion of applied linguistics as achieving a balance between expertise and experience. Do you consider the argument in this text to be maintaining such equilibrium, or does it tip the balance in favour of popular experience, unseating the authority of linguists completely?

▷ Cameron describes descriptivists as being in a 'finger-wagging tradition'. Is she not also 'finger wagging' or is that part of the point she is making?

Text 6

WILLIAM LABOV: 'The logic of nonstandard English' in Pier Paolo Giglioli (ed.): *Language and Social Context*. Penguin 1972, pages 179–80

In this text the sociolinguist William Labov argues against the idea that the language of some social groups is restricted or deficient. He goes on, in the later part of this paper—not quoted here—to suggest that such 'findings' are heavily influenced by the bias introduced when a working-class child is interviewed by a middle-class academic who speaks a very different variety of English. Properly understood, he argues, the language of disadvantaged black children was every bit as expressive as that of middle-class white children. (In this text he makes use of the now dated term 'Negro'.)

In the past decade, a great deal of federally sponsored research has been devoted to the educational problems of children in ghetto schools. In order to account for the poor performance of children in these schools, educational psychologists have attempted to discover what kind of disadvantage or defect they are suffering from. The viewpoint which has been widely accepted, and used as the basis for large-scale intervention programs, is that the children show a cultural deficit as a result of an impoverished environment in their early years. Considerable attention has been given to language. In this area, the deficit theory appears as the concept of 'verbal deprivation': Negro children from the ghetto receive little verbal stimulation, are said to hear very little well-formed language, and as a result are impoverished in their means of verbal expression: they cannot speak complete sentences, do not know the names of common objects, cannot form concepts or convey logical thoughts.

Unfortunately, these notions are based upon the work of educational psychologists who know very little about language and even less about Negro children. The concept of verbal deprivation has no basis in social reality: in fact, Negro children in the urban ghettos receive a great deal of verbal stimulation, hear more well-formed sentences than middle-class children, and participate fully in a highly verbal culture; they have the same basic vocabulary, possess the same capacity for conceptual learning, and use the same logic as anyone else who learns to speak and understand English.

The notion of 'verbal deprivation' is a part of the modern mythology of educational psychology, typical of the unfounded notions which tend to expand rapidly in our educational system. In past decades linguists have been as guilty as others in promoting such intellectual fashions at the expense of both teachers and children. But the myth of verbal deprivation is particularly dangerous, because it diverts attention from real defects of our educational system to imaginary defects of the child; and as we shall see, it leads its sponsors inevitably to the hypothesis of the genetic inferiority of Negro children which it was originally designed to avoid.

The most useful service which linguists can perform today is to clear away the illusion of 'verbal deprivation' and provide a more adequate notion of the relations between standard and nonstandard dialects. In the writings of many prominent educational psychologists, we find a very poor understanding of the nature of language.

▷ *Labov talks here about 'the myth of verbal deprivation' and suggests that it arises from 'a very poor understanding of the nature of language'. What do you think the author of Text 5 would say about this? Do you think Labov could be considered to be a finger-wagging descriptivist?*

Chapter 3
Languages in the contemporary world

Text 7
M.B.H.RAMPTON: 'Displacing the "native speaker":
expertise, affiliation, and inheritance'. *ELT Journal* 44/2,
1990, pages 97–8

*In this text Rampton argues that the term 'native speaker' is
as much political as linguistic and does not adequately
describe the nature of actual language users.*

In an educational context, the idea of being the native speaker of
a language and having it as your mother tongue tends to imply at
least five things:

1 A particular language is inherited, either through genetic
   endowment or through birth into the social group stereotypically
   associated with it.
2 Inheriting a language means being able to speak it well.
3 People either are or are not native/mother-tongue speakers.
4 Being a native speaker involves the comprehensive grasp of a
   language.
5 Just as people are usually citizens of one country, people are
   native speakers of one mother tongue.

All these connotations are now strongly contested by many
people. The capacity for language itself may be genetically
endowed, but *particular* languages are acquired in social settings.
It is sociolinguistically inaccurate to think of people belonging to
only one social group, once and for all. People participate in
many groups (the family, the peer group, and groups defined by
class, region, age, ethnicity, gender, etc.): membership changes
over time and so does language. Being born into a group does not
mean that you automatically speak its language well–many
native speakers of English can't write or tell stories, while many
non-native speakers can. Nobody's functional command is total:
users of a language are more proficient in some areas than others.
And most countries are multilingual: from an early age children
normally encounter two or more languages. Yet despite the
criticisms, the terms native speaker and mother tongue remain in

circulation, continuously insinuating their assumptions.

There are always ideological issues involved in discussions about who speaks what in education, and political interests often have a stake in maintaining the use of these concepts. Thus the supremacy of the native speaker keeps the UK and the US at the centre of ELT: at the opposite end of the scale, governments may use the notion of mother tongue to imply that certain languages are of interest only to particular minority groups, thereby denying either a language or its speakers full involvement in mainstream education. On its own, altering terminology does little to change this state of affairs, but by inserting or removing particular assumptions, alteration can clarify or usefully redirect our understanding.

▷ *Rampton suggests that it is wrong to assume that people either are or are not native speakers. What kind of intermediate cases do you think he is referring to?*

▷ *Does this text seem to be arguing for the abandonment of the term 'native speaker' altogether? Would it be possible, in your view, to discuss applied linguistic issues without this term, and if so what categories of speaker might replace it?*

Text 8

BARBARA SEIDLHOFER: 'Closing a conceptual gap: the case for a description of English as a lingua franca'. *International Journal of Applied Linguistics* 11/2, 2001, pages 151–2

This article discusses a rationale for a corpus compilation of English as a Lingua Franca (ELF) and points out how its findings might lead to a reconsideration of established ideas and attitudes about English as a property of its native speakers. In this extract Seidlhofer discusses aspects of the relation between ELF and English as a Native Language (ENL).

So how far any new findings will, or should, be acted upon is of course an open question. To be realistic, a linguistic innovation which goes against the grain of many people's tradition and etiquette is likely to meet with a great deal of resistance due to prejudice, market forces, vested interests, cultural sensibilities, aesthetic arguments and practical questions. But positive perspectives immediately arise as well: if recent important developments in applied linguistics on the meta-level are matched with an empirical basis for looking at the linguistic manifestations of ELF, this would help close the 'conceptual gap' I have discussed and provide us with a way of 'naming' ELF and making clear terminological distinctions.

There are also important advantages for ENL, and ENL speakers, in this: English as used by its native speakers has hitherto been faced with the impossible expectation that it should be 'all things to all people' and the inevitable failure in this has led to it (and its speakers) being subjected to accusations including those of contextual inappropriacy, cultural insensitivity and political imposition. At the same time, many native speakers of English feel that 'their language' is being abused and distorted through the diversity of its uses and users. If it becomes possible to call an instance of English use 'English as a lingua franca', analogous to, say, 'Nigerian English' and 'English English', this acts as a powerful signal that they are different 'territories' deserving mutual respect, and with their own 'legislation'. This would open up the possibility of engaging in 'code-switching' or at least 'concept-switching', and of an uninhibited acceptance of each use of 'English' in its own right—notably the appreciation of aesthetic and emotional aspects of literature, language play, rhetorical finesse, etc. Obviously, ENL would also remain intact as a target for learning in those circumstances where it is deemed appropriate. Most importantly perhaps, if ELF is conceptualised and accepted as a distinct manifestation of 'English' not tied to its native speakers, this opens up entirely new options for the way the world's majority of English teachers can perceive and define themselves: instead of being 'non-native' speakers and perennial learners of ENL, they can be competent and authoritative users of ELF. The 'native speaker teacher–non-native speaker teacher' dichotomy could then finally become obsolete in ELF settings, with the prospect of abolishing a counterproductive and divisive terminology which hinges on a negative particle, and which has bedevilled the profession for too long.

▷ *To what degree is the argument for ELF inevitably entailed by that in Text 7?*

▷ *Is it true, in your view, that speakers of English as a Native Language would also benefit from a change in attitude to ELF and ENL and the relationship between them?*

Text 9

ROBERT PHILLIPSON: *Linguistic Imperialism.*
Oxford University Press 1992, page 8

In the book from which this text is taken, Phillipson advances the view that the teaching of English cannot be regarded as politically neutral. It rather promotes the political interests of the USA and Britain, while at the same time hastening the decline of linguistic and cultural diversity.

In language pedagogy, the connections between the English language and political, economic, and military power are seldom pursued. Language pedagogy tends to focus on what goes on in the classroom, and related organizational and methodological matters. In professional English teaching circles, English tends to be regarded as an incontrovertible boon, as does language policy and pedagogy emanating from Britain and the USA. It is felt that while English was imposed by force in colonial times, contemporary language policies are determined by the state of the market ('demand') and the force of argument (rational planning in the light of the available 'facts'). The discourse accompanying and legitimating the export of English to the rest of the world has been so persuasive that English has been equated with progress and prosperity. In the view of the Ford Foundation's language projects officer, 'English as a Second Language (ESL) was believed to be a vital key to development by both the United States and by countries like Indonesia, the Philippines, Thailand, India, Turkey, Afghanistan, Pakistan, Egypt, Nigeria, Colombia, and Peru'. ...

The arguments in favour of English are intuitively commonsensical, but only in the Gramscian sense of being based on beliefs which reflect the dominant ideology ... . Hegemonic ideas tend to be internalized by the dominated, even though they are not objectively in their interest. Thus it will be seen that many of the tenets adhered to in educational language planning at the end of the colonial era, though apparently 'commonsensical', were scientifically fallacious ... . Similarly, many of the arguments used to promote English internationally are suspect, despite being intuitively sensible ... . Part of the explanation for this is that the majority of those working in the ELT field tend to confine themselves, by choice and training, to linguistic, literary, or pedagogical matters. ELT is however an international activity with political, economic, military, and cultural implications and ramifications.

▷ *In the other texts relating to this chapter, English is seen as—in one way or another—beyond the control of its native speakers. Is there a conflict between those views and that expressed here by Phillipson? Do you agree with him that the spread of a language can be equated with economic and military dominance, or are there important differences between these domains and the linguistic one?*

Chapter 4
English Language Teaching

Text 10

A.P.R.HOWATT: *A History of English Language Teaching.* Oxford University Press 1984, pages 192, 202–4

In this text the author groups a number of different approaches to language teaching together under a single heading. Firstly, he puts them in a historical context relating them to ideas which go back for several hundred years. Secondly, he relates them to the demographic and economic factors which led to their resurgence at the beginning of the twentieth century.

The communicative language teaching methods which have attracted a great deal of interest over the last ten years are the most recent manifestation of ideas that have appealed to the imagination of teachers for a very long time, and which were last revived about a hundred and twenty years ago by native-speaking immigrant teachers in America. These ideas have been known by a variety of labels (Natural Method, Conversation Method, Direct Method, Communicative Approach, and so on), and the classroom techniques associated with them have also changed from time to time. But the underlying philosophy has remained constant. Learning how to speak a new language, it is held, is not a rational process which can be organized in a step-by-step manner following graded syllabuses of new points to learn, exercises and explanations. It is an intuitive process for which human beings have a natural capacity that can be awakened provided only that the proper conditions exist. ...

'Natural methods' had started well and attracted professional interest and support. What they needed now was a vehicle which would bring them to the customers.

The ordinary schools of America, or anywhere else at the time, would never have adopted 'natural methods'. The teachers would not have known what to do, and parents would have been horrified at the loss of prestige that 'ordinary conversation' implied. Natural methods required schools of their own and someone with the feel for business to see and grasp the opportunity that was on offer. Immigrants were pouring into the United States speaking virtually every language in Europe and all of them needed to learn the language of their adopted country. But they were not an educated élite with years of the *Gymnasium*, the *lycée*, or whatever behind them. They were ordinary people, the poor, the dispossessed that passed under the Statue of Liberty in the steamships from Genoa and Hamburg. Like the Huguenots in sixteenth-century England, they needed to survive in their new environment and to cope with the problems of everyday life in a new language. They also brought with them their own natural skills as native speakers of their various languages. Someone who could put these two sets of needs and talents together in a system of language teaching that made no appeal to traditional scholastic knowledge but concentrated on what was actually wanted, would make his fortune. The moment found the man, in the shape of Maximilian Berlitz, appropriately enough an immigrant himself.

▷ *To what extent does this kind of explanation undermine the notion that approaches to language teaching are driven by new discoveries and ideas about how languages are acquired?*

▷ *Is there a note of irony in this text? If so, in which phrases is it located, and what kind of views are gently mocked?*

Text 11

PETER SKEHAN: *A Cognitive Approach to Language Learning*. Oxford University Press 1998, pages 3, 4

In this extract from the Introduction to this book, Skehan first sets out a number of assumptions about language learning which will guide his argument. He then moves on to outline an 'application' of these assumptions in language teaching. (The second application mentioned, to testing, is not covered in this text.)

If ... we have to regard second language learning as cognitive in orientation, then we need to take more seriously what psychologists tell us generally about how humans learn.

The second underlying assumption is less biological and more social and psychological. It is that *meaning* takes priority for older learners, and that the *form* of language has secondary importance. This claim relates to both comprehension and production. Regarding comprehension, the resources to extract meaning that humans possess increase in effectiveness as we get older. We become more adept at using strategies of communication, at exploiting schematic knowledge so that we say less but mean more, because we can exploit the collaborative construction of meaning that becomes increasingly possible. ...

Moving to production as language users, we develop effective means of coping with one of the greatest problems of all: how to keep speaking at normal rates in real time. We do this in a number of ways ... but one of the most important (in itself as well as for language learning) is that, as native speakers, we draw upon lexical modes of communication. In other words, rather than construct each utterance 'mint fresh' ..., we economize by stitching together language chunks which free processing resources during communication so that planning for the form and content of future utterances can proceed more smoothly. ...

When we turn to learning and change, the analysis becomes even more intriguing. ... methods of contriving a focus on form are needed which capture learners' attention, so that they may incorporate newly-noticed forms into their developing language systems.

Task-based instruction and language testing

Following from such general discussion of psycholinguistic influences on performance and learning, two major practical applications are offered: towards task-based instruction and towards language testing. Much foreign language instruction is based on form-focused language presentation, followed by controlled practice. Only then is some degree of free production used. A task-based approach, in contrast, gives learners tasks to transact in the expectation that doing such tasks, for example, comparing one another's family trees, will drive forward language development. Given that language is learned for communication, and that meaning is primary, the attraction of a task-based approach to instruction is that it enables each of these to operate fairly directly. But of course the disadvantage is that engaging meaning and enabling communication might de-emphasize form even further than might be the case otherwise. So the challenge of task-based instruction is to contrive sufficient focus on form to enable interlanguage development to proceed without compromising the naturalness of the communication that tasks can generate.

▷ *In this text, change in language-teaching practice is seen as driven by changes in theories of language and language acquisition. To what degree is such an approach compatible with that in Text 10, where change is explained in terms of social and economic factors in the world at large?*

▷ *Skehan seems to imply that successful 'lexical modes of communication' are a distinctive quality of being a 'native speaker'. Is this view at odds with those in Texts 7 and 8?*

▷ *If the assumptions described in the first part of this text were shown to be wrong, would the case for TBI in the second part then collapse, or would TBI still be valid for other reasons?*

Text 12
H.G.WIDDOWSON: 'The ownership of English'.
TESOL Quarterly 28/2, 1994, pages 388–9

At the end of this influential paper arguing that English can no longer be considered the property of the inner-circle countries, the author argues that approaches valid in one pedagogic context cannot necessarily be generalized to all others.

So it is that native speakers write textbooks and teachers' books, make pronouncements and recommendations, and bring to remote and hitherto benighted places the good news about real English and good teaching to lighten their darkness. Real English: their English. Good teaching: their teaching. But both are contextually limited by cultural factors. Their English is that which is associated with the communicative and communal needs of their community, and these may have little relevance for those learning English as an international language.

And their teaching is suited to particular contexts of instruction which in many respects are quite different from those which obtain in the world at large. Consider, for example, a language school in England, with English as the ambient language outside the classroom, the students well off and well motivated, but quite different in linguistic and cultural background both from each other, and from the teacher. In such a context it is, of course, necessary to focus on what can be established as a common denominator. Everybody is here in England, for example, and everybody is human. And so you devise an approach to teaching which combines authenticity with an appeal to universal natural learning and humanistic response. This is an example of appropriate pedagogy: Such an approach is necessary and of course it works in these local conditions. Highly commendable. But it is exclusive in that it excludes possibilities which might be particularly appropriate elsewhere—translation, for example. The problem is when an absolute virtue is made of local necessity by claims of global validity, when it is assumed that if the approach works here it ought to work, or be made to work, everywhere else. This is a denial of diversity.

For of course there is no reason why it should work elsewhere where quite different conditions obtain. It is difficult to resist the conclusion that such an approach, which makes a virtue of necessity, is only privileged because of the authority vested in the teachers by virtue of their native-speaker status. This is not to say that it may not offer ideas worth pondering, but then these ideas have to be analysed out of the approach and their relevance evaluated in reference to other contexts. You should not assume, with bland arrogance, that your way of teaching English, or your way of using English, carries a general guarantee of quality. To put the point briefly: English and English teaching are proper to the extent that they are appropriate, not to the extent that they are appropriated.

▷ *Is one of the implications of this argument that the shift from grammar-translation to direct method described in Text 10 was only valid in a particular time and place?*

▷ *At the end of this text, Widdowson refers to the 'bland arrogance' of those who assume that their 'way of teaching English' will be relevant in all times and all places. To what degree does this apply to all the various approaches to TEFL described in Chapter 4?*

Chapter 5
Language and communication

Text 13
DELL HYMES: 'On communicative competence' in J.B. Pride and J. Holmes (eds.): *Sociolinguistics*. Penguin 1972, pages 6, 14–15

In this extract from the opening pages of his very influential article, Hymes points out the limitations of a theoretical perspective (that of Chomsky) that defines competence as a knowledge of grammatical sentences, and puts forward the alternative notion of 'communicative competence' as accounting more fully for the child's experience of language.

The special relevance of the theoretical perspective is expressed in … the image it puts before our eyes. The image is that of a child, born with the ability to master any language with almost miraculous ease and speed; a child who is not merely molded by conditioning and reinforcement, but who actively proceeds with the unconscious theoretical interpretation of the speech that comes its way, so that in a few years and with a finite experience, it is master of an infinite ability, that of producing and understanding in principle any and all grammatical sentences of language. The image (or theoretical perspective) expresses the essential equality in children just as human beings. It is noble in that it can inspire one with the belief that even the most dispiriting conditions can be transformed; it is an indispensable weapon against views that would explain the communicative differences among groups of children as inherent, perhaps racial.

The limitations of the perspective appear when the image of the unfolding, mastering, fluent child is set beside the real children in our schools. The theory must seem, if not irrelevant, then at best a doctrine of poignancy: poignant, because of the difference between what one imagines and what one sees; poignant too, because the theory, so powerful in its own realm, cannot on its terms cope with the difference. To cope with the realities of children as communicating beings requires a theory within which sociocultural factors have an explicit and constitutive role; and neither is the case. ...

Recall that one is concerned to explain how a child comes rapidly to be able to produce and understand (in principle) any and all of the grammatical sentences of a language. Consider now a child with just that ability. A child who might produce any sentence whatever—such a child would be likely to be institutionalized: even more so if not only sentences, but also speech or silence was random, unpredictable. For that matter, a person who chooses occasions and sentences suitably, but is master only of fully grammatical sentences, is at best a bit odd. Some occasions call for being appropriately ungrammatical.

We have then to account for the fact that a normal child acquires knowledge of sentences, not only as grammatical, but also as appropriate. He or she acquires competence as to when to speak, when not, and as to what to talk about with whom, when, where, in what manner. In short, a child becomes able to accomplish a repertoire of speech acts, to take part in speech events, and to evaluate their accomplishment by others. This competence, moreover, is integral with attitudes, values, and motivations concerning language, its features and uses, and integral with competence for, and attitudes toward, the interrelation of language with the other code of communicative conduct.

▷ *Hymes' view of communicative competence is often represented*
as a complete rejection of Chomsky's account of competence.
Does this text bear out this interpretation of Hymes' position?

Text 14
MICHAEL CANALE and MERRILL SWAIN: 'Theoretical bases
of communicative approaches to second language teaching
and testing'. *Applied Linguistics* 1/1, 1980, pages 28–31

In this influential article, Canale and Swain set out an
alternative model of communicative competence to that of
Hymes. The extract below describes and defines the
components of the new model: grammatical competence,
sociolinguistic competence (subdivided into sociocultural
competence and discourse competence), and strategic com-
petence.

A proposed theoretical framework for communicative competence

Our own tentative theory of communicative competence minimally
includes three main competencies: grammatical competence,
sociolinguistic competence, and strategic competence. The purpose
of this section is to briefly outline the contents and boundaries of
each of these areas of competence. ...

Grammatical competence. This type of competence will be
understood to include knowledge of lexical items and of rules
of morphology, syntax, sentence-grammar semantics, and
phonology. ...

Sociolinguistic competence. This component is made up of two
sets of rules: sociocultural rules of use and rules of discourse. ...
   Sociocultural rules of use will specify the ways in which
utterances are produced and understood *appropriately* with respect
to the components of communicative events outlined by Hymes ... .
The primary focus of these rules is on the extent to which certain
propositions and communicative functions are appropriate within
a given sociocultural context depending on contextual factors such
as topic, role of participants, setting, and norms of interaction. A

secondary concern of such rules is the extent to which appropriate attitude and register or style are conveyed by a particular grammatical form within a given sociocultural context. For example, it would generally be inappropriate for a waiter in a restaurant to actually command a client to order a certain menu item, regardless of how the proposition and communicative function were expressed grammatically; likewise, inappropriate attitude and register would be expressed if a waiter in a tasteful restaurant were to ask, 'O.K., chump, what are you and this broad gonna eat?' in taking an order. ...

... the focus of rules of discourse in our framework is the combination of utterances and communicative functions and not the grammatical well-formedness of a single utterance nor the sociocultural appropriateness of a set of propositions and communicative functions in a given context. ...

Strategic competence. This component will be made up of verbal and non-verbal communication strategies that may be called into action to compensate for breakdowns in communication due to performance variables or to insufficient competence. Such strategies will be of two main types: those that relate primarily to grammatical competence (e.g. how to paraphrase grammatical forms that one has not mastered or cannot recall momentarily) and those that relate more to sociolinguistic competence (e.g. various role-playing strategies, how to address strangers when unsure of their social status).

▷ *How do these components of communicative competence relate to those of Hymes' model (possibility, feasibility, appropriateness, and attestedness)? Has anything disappeared, and is there anything completely new?*

▷ *Does this new model have any implications for teaching which Hymes' model does not?*

Chapter 6
Context and culture

Text 15
CLAIRE KRAMSCH: *Context and Culture in Language Teaching*. Oxford University Press 1993, pages 8,9

In this book, Kramsch argues for a more central place for culture in language teaching. She sees the classroom, however, not simply as the meeting place of cultures (the learner's and that of the language being taught) but as the place in which there emerges a more complex 'third culture in its own right'.

The same hesitation about the teaching of literature in language classes can be found with the teaching of culture. One often reads in teachers' guide-lines that language teaching consists of teaching the four skills 'plus culture'. This dichotomy of language and culture is an entrenched feature of language teaching around the world. It is part of the linguistic heritage of the profession. Whether it is called (Fr.) *civilisation*, (G.) *Landeskunde*, or (Eng.) *culture*, culture is often seen as mere information conveyed by the language, not as a feature of language itself; cultural awareness becomes an educational objective in itself, separate from language. If, however, language is seen as social practice, culture becomes the very core of language teaching. Cultural awareness must then be viewed both as enabling language proficiency and as being the outcome of reflection on language proficiency. ...

The question that concerns us here is the following: given that we want to teach language in such a way that learners are initiated into its social and cultural meanings, how many of these meanings must be made explicit, how many can be understood implicitly? How can a foreign way of viewing the world be taught via an educational culture which is itself the product of native conceptions and values? Once we recognize that language use is indissociable from the creation and transmission of culture, we have to deal with a variety of cultures, some more international than others, some more conventionalized than others. ...

For research purposes, it has been customary to view the linguistic development of a learner on an interlanguage continuum whose endpoint is a linguistic construct called the 'native speaker'. Non-native teachers and students alike are intimidated by the native-speaker norm and understandably try to approximate this norm during the course of their work together. If, however, we consider language study as initiation into a kind of social practice that is at the boundary of two or more cultures, such a linear progression makes less sense. In fact what is at stake is the creation, in and through the classroom, of a social, linguistic reality that is born from the L1 [first-language] speech environment of the learners and the social environment of the L2 [second-language] native speakers, but is a third culture in its own right.

▷ *What are your answers to the questions Kramsch asks in the penultimate paragraph of this text?*

▷ *Do these arguments, in your view, apply equally to the teaching of all languages, and in all circumstances?*

▷ *How do you think Kramsch's ideas would fit into the notion of communicative competence outlined in Text 14?*

Chapter 7
Persuasion and poetics; rhetoric and resistance

Text 16
ROGER FOWLER: *Linguistic Criticism* (2nd edn.). Oxford University Press 1996, pages 63, 64–5

In this text, Fowler, one of the founders of critical linguistics, considers how language is used to create special effects in the lines of a poem by William Carlos Williams.

> Why bother where I went?
> for I went spinning on the
>
> four wheels of my car
> along the wet road until
>
> I saw a girl with one leg
> over the rail of a balcony

Like the car driver who when he is moving glimpses an object from one position then from another, so that the object changes, the reader first assumes that the penultimate line refers to an amputee, and then as he shifts his attention to the last line is forced to reinterpret completely, restoring the leg. The switch from one interpretation to the other is striking partly because it so neatly mimes a visual process appropriate to the narrative of the poem. ...

... This is a very radical kind of defamiliarization which, by insisting that a sign is not tied to *one* meaning, constitutes a critique of the conventionality of signs.

The technique by which William Carlos Williams achieves this particular act of defamiliarization is very simple in its design, quite complicated in its execution. In verse, the sequence of words and phrases can be divided up in two ways. There are the normal syntactic boundaries:

between words:

> my / car

between phrases:

> on the four wheels / of my car

between clauses:

> for I went spinning on the four wheels of my car along the wet road / until I saw a girl with one leg over the rail of a balcony

between sentences:

> Why bother where I went? / for I went *etc.*

These syntactic divisions have an intuitive psychological reality for speakers of a language, and are felt to divide up the flow of words into units of meaning. There is a second set of segmentations in verse, the line-divisions. ... Now if the last word in a line *could* be the last word of a syntactic unit, the line-ending encourages the reader to assume that the syntax *does* end there.

▷ *How does this account of two ways of dividing up the sequence of words and phrases point to the poet's technique for achieving defamiliarization?*

▷ *Fowler says that such defamiliarization 'constitutes a critique of the conventionality of signs'. What do you think he means by that?*

Text 17

NORMAN FAIRCLOUGH and RUTH WODAK: 'Critical Discourse Analysis' in Teun A. van Dijk (ed.): *Discourse as Social Interaction*. SAGE Publications 1997, pages 258–9

This text, by two of the leading figures in critical discourse analysis, gives a clear and accessible introduction to the movement's main principles.

Like other approaches to discourse analysis, critical discourse analysis (henceforth CDA) analyses real and often extended instances of social interaction which take a linguistic form, or a partially linguistic form. The critical approach is distinctive in its view of (a) the relationship between language and society, and (b) the relationship between analysis and the practices analysed. Let us take these in turn.

CDA sees discourse–language use in speech and writing—as a form of 'social practice'. Describing discourse as social practice implies a dialectical relationship between a particular discursive event and the situation(s), institution(s) and social structure(s) which frame it. A dialectical relationship is a two-way relationship: the discursive event is shaped by situations, institutions and social structures, but it also shapes them. To put the same point in a different way, discourse is socially *constitutive* as well as socially shaped: it constitutes situations, objects of knowledge, and the social identities of and relationships between people and groups of people. It is constitutive both in the sense that it helps to sustain and reproduce the social status quo, and in the sense that it contributes to transforming it. Since discourse is so socially influential, it gives rise to important issues of power. Discursive practices may have major ideological effects: that is, they can help produce and reproduce unequal power relations between (for instance) social classes, women and men, and ethnic/cultural majorities and minorities through the ways in which they represent things and position people. So discourse may, for example, be racist, or sexist, and try to pass off assumptions (often falsifying ones) about any aspect of social life as mere common sense. Both the ideological loading of particular ways of using language and the relations of power which underlie them are often unclear to people. CDA aims to make more visible these opaque aspects of discourse.

CDA sees itself not as dispassionate and objective social science, but as engaged and committed. It is a form of intervention in social practice and social relationships: many analysts are politically active against racism, or as feminists, or within the peace movement, and so forth. But CDA is not an exception to the normal objectivity of social science: social science is inherently tied into politics and formulations of policy, as for instance Foucault's ... work convincingly demonstrated. What is distinctive about CDA is both that it intervenes on the side of dominated and oppressed groups and against dominating groups, and that it openly declares the emancipatory interests that motivate it. The political interests and uses of social scientific research are usually less explicit. This certainly does not imply that CDA is less scholarly than other research: standards of careful, rigorous and systematic analysis apply with equal force to CDA as to other approaches.

▷ *Is there a contradiction between the claims that 'CDA sees itself not as dispassionate and objective social science' and 'CDA is not an exception to the normal objectivity of social science'?*

▷ *How far do you think the view expressed here relates to the notion of defamiliarization as discussed in Text 16?*

Chapter 8
Past, present, and future directions

Text 18
ROSAMUND MITCHELL and FLORENCE MYLES: *Second Language Learning Theories*. Arnold 1998, page 195

In this text, extracted from their authoritative survey of SLA research, the authors reflect upon the relationship between theories of SLA and foreign language teaching.

The findings of SLA research are not sufficiently secure, clear and uncontested, across broad enough domains, to provide straight-forward prescriptive guidance for the teacher (nor, perhaps, will they ever be so). They are not generally presented and disseminated in ways accessible and meaningful to teachers; the agenda of SLA research does not necessarily centre on the issues which teachers are most conscious of as problematic. But most importantly, teaching is an art as well as a science, and irreducibly so, because of the constantly varying nature of the classroom as a learning community. There can be no 'one best method', however much research evidence supports it, which applies at all times and in all situations, with every type of learner. Instead, teachers 'read' and interpret the changing dynamics of the learning context from moment to moment, and take what seem to them to be appropriate contingent actions, in the light of largely implicit, proceduralized pedagogic knowledge. This has been built up over time very largely from their own previous experience, and usually derives only to a much more limited extent from study or from organized training.

However, present SLA research offers a rich variety of concepts and descriptive accounts, which can help teachers interpret and make better sense of their own classroom experiences, and significantly broaden the range of pedagogic choices open to them. For example, SLL [Second-Language Learning] research has produced descriptive accounts of the course of interlanguage development, which show that learners follow relatively invariant routes of learning, but that such routes are not linear, including phases of restructuring and apparent regression. Such accounts have helped teachers to understand patterns of learner error and its inevitability, and more generally, to accept the indirect nature of the relationship between what is taught and what is learned. Similarly, in the recent literature, discussions about the role of recasts and negative evidence in learning ..., about scaffolding and microgenesis ..., or about language socialization ... have great potential to stimulate teacher reflections on the discourse choices available to them, when enacting their own role as L2 [second-language] guide and interlocutor.

Of course, the subfield of research on 'instructed SLA' ... plays a special role in addressing concerns somewhat closer to those of the classroom teacher, and may offer opportunities for more direct involvement of teachers as research partners. But even 'instructed SLA' research is not identical with problem-solving and development in language pedagogy, and does not ensure a shared agenda between teachers and researchers. There is a continuing need for dialogue between the 'practical theories' of classroom educators, and the more decontextualized and abstract ideas deriving from programmes of research. Researchers thus have a continuing responsibility to make their findings and their interpretations of them as intelligible as possible to a wider professional audience, with other preoccupations.

▷ *Mitchell and Myles here write that 'There can be no "one best method" however much research evidence supports it'. Is this at odds with the argument of Text 11?*

▷ *Is the implication of this text that some SLA research is 'linguistics applied', some is 'applied linguistics', and some is just 'linguistics'?*

Text 19

SUSAN HUNSTON: *Corpora in Applied Linguistics.*
Cambridge University Press 2002, pages 3, 13–14

In this text, Hunston discusses the application of corpus find-ings across a wide range of applied linguistic areas, including language teaching, translation, clinical and forensic linguistics, and cultural studies.

What a corpus can do

Strictly speaking, a corpus by itself can do nothing at all, being nothing other than a store of used language. Corpus access software, however, can re-arrange that store so that observations of various kinds can be made. If a corpus represents, very roughly and partially, a speaker's experience of language, the access software re-orders that experience so that it can be examined in ways that are usually impossible. A corpus does not contain new information about language, but the software offers us a new perspective on the familiar. Most readily available software packages process data from a corpus in three ways: showing frequency, phraseology, and collocation. ...

What corpora are used for

Corpora nowadays have a diverse range of uses ...
- For language teaching, corpora can give information about how a language works that may not be accessible to native speaker intuition, such as ... detailed phraseology ... . In addition, the relative frequency of different features can be calculated. ... for example, nearly all the future time reference in conversational English is indicated by *will* or other modals. The phrase *BE going to* accounts for about 10% of future time reference, and the present progressive less than 5%. Information such as this is important for syllabus and materials design.
- Increasingly, language classroom teachers are encouraging students to explore corpora for themselves ..., allowing them to observe nuances of usage and to make comparisons between languages.
- Translators use comparable corpora to compare the use of apparent translation equivalents in two languages, and parallel corpora to see how words and phrases have been translated in the past. ... for example, the English word *still* can translate or be translated by the French *toujours* or *encore*, or by expressions with *couramment* or the verb *continuer*. Sometimes when an English sentence includes the word *still* the parallel French sentence has no translation equivalent at all, but when *toujours* and *encore* are present in the French sentence, the English parallel sentence always contains *still*.
- General corpora can be used to establish norms of frequency and usage against which individual texts can be measured. This has applications for work in stylistics and in clinical and forensic linguistics.
- Corpora are used also to investigate cultural attitudes expressed through language ... and as a resource for crucial discourse studies ... .

▷ *In what ways do you think the kind of findings described or suggested here might change the practice of teachers, translators, speech therapists, and other language professionals?*

Text 20

ALASTAIR PENNYCOOK: *Critical Applied Linguistics: A Critical Introduction*. Lawrence Erlbaum Associates 2001, pages 4, 5, 9

This text indicates some of the distinctive features of CALx.

Although there is of course much to be said for ... an ability to analyze and critique, there are two other major themes in critical work that sit in opposition to this approach. The first may accept the possibility that critical distance and objectivity are important and achievable but argues that the most significant aspect of critical work is an engagement with political critiques of social relations. Such a position insists that critical inquiry can remain objective and is no less so because of its engagement with social critique. The second argument is one that also insists on the notion of *critical* as always engaging with questions of power and inequality, but it differs from the first in terms of its rejection of any possibility of critical distance or objectivity. ...

It is common to view applied linguistics as concerned with language in context, but the conceptualization of context is frequently one that is limited to an overlocalized and under-theorized view of social relations. One of the key challenges for critical applied linguistics, therefore, is to find ways of mapping micro and macro relations, ways of understanding a relation between concepts of society, ideology, global capitalism, colonialism, education, gender, racism, sexuality, class, and classroom utterances, translations, conversations, genres, second language acquisition, media texts. Whether it is critical applied linguistics as a critique of mainstream applied linguistics, or as a form of critical text analysis, or as an approach to understanding the politics of translation, or as an attempt to understand implications of the global spread of English, a central issue always concerns how the classroom, text, or conversation is related to broader social cultural and political relations. ...

Rampton ... argues that applied linguistics in Britain has started to shift from its 'autonomous' view of research with connections to pedagogy, linguistics, and psychology to a more 'ideological' model with connections to media studies and a more grounded understanding of social processes. Critical applied linguistics opens the door for such change even wider by drawing on yet another range of 'outside' work (critical theory, feminism, postcolonialism, poststructuralism, antiracist pedagogy) that both challenges and greatly enriches the possibilities for doing applied linguistics. This means not only that critical applied linguistics implies a hybrid model of research and praxis but also that it generates something that is far more dynamic. As with the notion of synergy as the productive melding of two elements to create something larger than the sum of its parts, I am using here the notion of heterosis as the creative expansion of possibilities resulting from hybridity. Put more simply, my point here is that critical applied linguistics is far more than the addition of a critical dimension to applied linguistics; rather, it opens up a whole new array of questions and concerns, issues such as identity, sexuality, or the reproduction of Otherness that have hitherto not been considered as concerns related to applied linguistics.

▷ *How far are the ideas expressed in this text consistent with those expressed in Text 17?*

▷ *Pennycook claims that critical applied linguistics 'opens up a whole new array of questions and concerns'. What do you think these might be? Which, in your view, could not be addressed by applied linguistics as defined in Text 1?*

References

The references which follow can be classified into introductory level (marked ■□□), more advanced and consequently more technical (marked ■■□), and specialized, very demanding (marked ■■■).

Chapter 1
Applied linguistics

■■□

ALAN DAVIES: *An Introduction to Applied Linguistics.* Edinburgh University Press 1999

This survey of the field takes the view that an understanding of applied linguistics best emerges from engaging in practice first and theory later. The book includes interesting accounts of the history and development of applied linguistics.

■■□

GUY COOK and BARBARA SEIDLHOFER (eds.): *Principle and Practice in Applied Linguistics.* Oxford University Press 1995

This collection of essays by leading applied linguists covers a wide range of issues and activities in the contemporary field.

■■□

CHRISTOPHER BRUMFIT: *Individual Freedom in Language Teaching.* Oxford University Press 2001

This is an inspiring book in which the author addresses, in characteristically engaging manner, a very wide range of issues which relate to language pedagogy and are of general relevance to applied linguistics.

■□□

KEITH JOHNSON and HELEN JOHNSON (eds.):
Encyclopaedic Dictionary of Applied Linguistics.
Blackwell 1998

Aimed primarily at those concerned with language teaching, this is a useful reference book, clearly summarizing key concepts and areas of research and practice.

■■□

MICHAEL MCCARTHY: *Issues in Applied Linguistics.*
Cambridge University Press 2001

This is a stimulating and engaging discussion of six central areas of controversy and debate in contemporary applied linguistics.

Chapter 2
Prescribing and describing: popular and academic views of 'correctness'

■■□

DEBORAH CAMERON: *Verbal Hygiene.* Routledge 1995

This is a fascinating and readable survey of the many reasons why people try to regulate the use of language and prescribe both what should and what should not be said or written. Rather than dismissing prescriptivism, however, the author argues that it should in itself be an area of linguistic enquiry.

■■□

TONY BEX and RICHARD WATTS (eds.): *Standard English: The Widening Debate.* Routledge 1999

This is an up-to-date and wide-ranging collection of papers which examines current debate over standard English from historical, sociolinguistic, descriptive, and educational perspectives.

Chapter 3
Languages in the contemporary world

■■□

ROBERT PHILLIPSON: *Linguistic Imperialism.*
Oxford University Press 1992

The book expounds, with detailed documentation, the view that
ELT both promotes the political and economic aims of the inner-
circle English-speaking countries and damages the interests and
identities of other languages and cultures.

■□□

DAVID CRYSTAL: *English as a Global Language.*
Canto 1997

This is a brief but very informative introductory survey of the extent
and nature of English as a global language in the contemporary
world.

■□□

DAVID GRADDOL: *The Future of English.*
The British Council 1997

Like Crystal's book, this provides an analysis of the current state
of English in the world. It also speculates upon its possible future
development. It is a more critical and political, and less optimistic,
account than Crystal's.

■■□

JENNIFER JENKINS: *The Phonology of English as an
International Language.* Oxford University Press 2000

This book advocates and explores a non-native model of English
for pronunciation teaching in which the goal is mutual
intelligibility rather than conformity to native-speaker norms. It
thus develops in detail the implications of the notion of English
as a lingua franca.

Chapter 4
English Language Teaching

■■☐

H.G. WIDDOWSON: *Defining Issues in English Language Teaching.* Oxford University Press 2003

This is an up-to-date, authoritative, and engaging discussion, based upon the author's papers and articles from the 1990s and 2000s, of major issues in applied linguistics and ELT. It is similar in approach and spirit to earlier collections by the same author: *Explorations in Applied Linguistics* (1979); *Explorations in Applied Linguistics 2* (1984); and *Aspects of Language Teaching* (1990).

■☐☐

KEITH JOHNSON: *An Introduction to Foreign Language Learning and Teaching.* Longman 2001

This is a readable and accessible survey of the state of contemporary language teaching. It provides an even-handed description of a variety of approaches, a discussion of major issues, and a useful historical survey of their origins.

■■☐

A.P.R. HOWATT: *A History of English Language Teaching.* Oxford University Press 1984

This authoritative and comprehensive history is a unique book of great intrinsic interest. It serves the useful function of setting current fashions in a wider historical context, enabling the reader to see their relationship to social, political, and demographic change, as well as to wider intellectual currents, and changes in theories of language and language acquisition.

■■☐

H.H. STERN: *Issues and Options in Language Teaching.* Oxford University Press 1992

This book analyses the choices confronted by language teachers, relating them to applied linguistic theory and research. It moves from the general to the particular, considering language teaching policy, objectives, content, and strategies.

■■□

GUY COOK: *Language Play, Language Learning.*
Oxford University Press 2000

This book contests the assumption that the main function of language is the transaction of information, arguing that language play (defined as the patterning of form, the creation of alternative worlds, and the use of language for social inclusion and exclusion) is at least equally important. The last two chapters criticize the view that language learning is best effected through 'real', meaningful, and work-oriented language and activity.

■■□

MARTIN BYGATE, PETER SKEHAN, and MERRILL SWAIN (eds.): *Researching Pedagogic Tasks*. Longman 2001

This book brings together accounts of empirical studies into the use of tasks for second language learning, relating the problems of practical implementation to relevant theories of language learning.

■■□

PETER SKEHAN: *A Cognitive Approach to Language Learning.* Oxford University Press 1998

This is a detailed exposition of recent research and ideas from SLA and psycholinguistics. It argues for task-based instruction in language teaching.

Chapter 5
Language and communication

■■□

DELL HYMES: 'On communicative competence' in J.B. Pride and J. Holmes (eds.): *Sociolinguistics*. Penguin 1972

This much-cited text sets out in detail Hymes' model of communicative competence (as described and analysed in Chapter 5).

■■■

MICHAEL CANALE and MERRILL SWAIN: 'Theoretical bases of communicative approaches to second language teaching and testing'. *Applied Linguistics* 1/1, 1980

Building upon Hymes' original model, this influential article develops an alternative model of communicative competence which, while keeping Hymes' main idea, suggests a different set of parameters.

■■■

H.G. WIDDOWSON: 'Knowledge of language and ability for use'. *Applied Linguistics* 10/2, 1989

This influential paper argues that knowledge of communicative competence does not necessarily entail the ability to put this knowledge to effective use, and that the two should therefore be treated as separate aspects of communicative competence. The issue of the journal *Applied Linguistics* in which it appears is devoted to the topic of communicative competence.

Chapter 6
Context and culture

■□□

GUY COOK: *Discourse*, in the series 'Language Teaching, a Scheme for Teacher Education'. Oxford University Press 1989

Section One of this book provides an overview of approaches to discourse analysis. Sections Two and Three relate these to the concerns of language teachers.

■■□

RONALD CARTER and MICHAEL MCCARTHY: *Language as Discourse*. Longman 1994

This book provides an accessible and clearly written introduction to discourse analysis, exploring the relationship between complete texts, both spoken and written, and the social and cultural contexts in which they function. In the light of this discussion, the authors argue that language teachers, syllabus designers, and curriculum organizers should give greater attention to language as discourse.

■■□

GUNTHER KRESS and THEO VAN LEEUWEN: *Reading Images: The Grammar of Visual Design*. Routledge 1996

This innovative book examines the differences and similarities between visual and linguistic communication, as well as ways in which each is used to enhance the other. It discusses the formal elements and structures of visual design, including the uses of colour, framing, and composition, with reference to a very wide range of examples.

■□□

JENNY THOMAS: *Meaning in Interaction*. Longman 1995

This is a brief and very readable introduction to the field of pragmatics. It is illustrated with interesting and often amusing examples from the author's own collection of data.

■□□

DAVID CRYSTAL: *Language and the Internet*. Cambridge University Press 2001

This is a readable and comprehensive overview of the use of language in computer-mediated communication (although it does not itself use the term).

Chapter 7
Persuasion and poetics; rhetoric and resistance

■■■

JEAN-JACQUES WEBER (ed.): *The Stylistics Reader*. Arnold 1996

This is an anthology of classic and seminal papers in literary stylistics, each paired with a more recent critical response.

■■□

RONALD CARTER and JOHN MCRAE (eds.): *Language, Literature and the Learner: Creative Classroom Practice.* Longman 1996

A collection of papers exploring the application of insights from literary stylistics in literature and language teaching.

■■□

H.G. WIDDOWSON: *Stylistics and the Teaching of Literature.* Longman 1975

In this book, the author sets out the principles of literary stylistics as an endeavour mediating between linguistic description and literary criticism. It remains the clearest and most accessible introduction to literary stylistics and its relevance to teaching.

■■□

H.G. WIDDOWSON: *Practical Stylistics.* Oxford University Press 1992

In this book, the author explores how students' awareness of linguistic detail in literary texts can be developed through a series of practical activities which involve manipulating and rewriting poems.

■■□

DEBORAH CAMERON: *Good to Talk? Living and Working in a Communication Culture.* SAGE Publications 2000

A critical examination of 'language work' in contemporary society, focusing upon the control of employees' language use by employers. It provides an excellent example of how language research can be made relevant to pressing contemporary concerns.

■■□

NORMAN FAIRCLOUGH: *Language and Power* (2nd edn.). Routledge 2001

This is the seminal work on critical discourse analysis, now in a second edition. It seeks to show how language maintains and changes power relations, and how analysis can, by raising awareness, make readers more able to resist manipulation.

Chapter 8
Past, present, and future directions

■■□

ROSAMOND MITCHELL and FLORENCE MYLES:
Second Language Learning Theories. Arnold 1998

This is an accessible survey of a wide range of theories and approaches to the study of second language learning. The authors cover a wide variety of approaches, giving a clear and fair account of each one.

■■■

ROD ELLIS: *The Study of Second Language Acquisition.*
Oxford University Press 1994.

This book provides a very detailed account of SLA research up to the date of publication. At over 800 pages it is an invaluable reference book for those seeking a comprehensive knowledge of the field.

■■□

SUSAN HUNSTON: *Corpora in Applied Linguistics.*
Cambridge University Press 2002

This is a clear, up-to-date, and authoritative account of corpus linguistics, and the relevance and application of its findings to language teaching and other applied linguistic activity.

■■□

ALASTAIR PENNYCOOK: *Critical Applied Linguistics:
A Critical Introduction.* Lawrence Erlbaum Associates 2001

This is a clearly written exposition of the author's programme for a politically committed applied linguistics, making reference to a wide range of work from relevant disciplines and commenting upon how the proposed new programme both draws upon, and differs from, existing work in the field.

SECTION 4
Glossary

Page references to Section 1, Survey, are given at the end of each entry.

additional-language education The study of a language which is not a person's home or main language or languages. [7]

applied linguistics The academic discipline concerned with the relation of knowledge about language to decision making in the real world. [5]

appropriateness Knowledge of whether and to what degree verbal or non-verbal behaviour is appropriate to a particular situation, relationship, culture, or **genre**. (The third parameter of Hymes' model of communicative competence.) [42]

attestedness Knowledge of whether and to what degree a particular combination of words actually occurs. (The fourth parameter of Hymes' model of communicative competence.) [42]

CALx *See* **Critical Applied Linguistics.**

CDA *See* **Critical Discourse Analysis.**

clinical linguistics The study and treatment of speech and communication impairments, whether hereditary, developmental, or acquired. [7]

CLT *See* **Communicative Language Teaching.**

CMC *See* **Computer-Mediated Communication.**

code-switching Changing back and forth between two languages, or two varieties of the same language. [24]

collocation A frequent combination of words, e.g. 'provide assistance'. [73]

communicative approach An approach to language teaching which views the ability to communicate successfully as both the means and the end of language learning. [36, 46]

communicative competence The knowledge which is necessary to use a language effectively, and the ability to put that knowledge into action. [42]

Communicative Language Teaching (CLT) The implementation of the **communicative approach** in syllabuses, materials, and classroom practice. [36]

competence *See* **linguistic competence.** [9]

Computer-Mediated Communication (CMC) Communication via a computer network. It may be one-to-one or one-to-many, and synchronous (in which participants are on-line simultaneously) or asynchronous (in which they are on-line at different times). [51]

context Factors outside a stretch of language under consideration but relevant to its interpretation, e.g. the situation, paralinguistic communication, cultural knowledge, other texts, or other parts of the same text. [49]

conversationalization The contemporary tendency for all communication to adopt the conventions of one-to-one, face-to-face interaction between equals. (A term first used by Norman Fairclough.) [67]

corpus linguistics The systematic analysis and description of extensive databanks of language which has actually occurred in use. [9, 46, 73]

Critical Applied Linguistics (CALx) A politically committed approach to **applied linguistics** claiming to combat injustice and inequality. [75]

Critical Discourse Analysis (CDA) The study of the relationship between linguistic choices and effects in persuasive uses of language, of how these indoctrinate or manipulate (e.g. in marketing and politics), and the counteracting of this through analysis. [8, 65]

critical linguistics The investigation of the relation between linguistic choices and ideology. [65]

cross-cultural communication The study of the problems and misunderstandings which arise in communication when people assume different cultural conventions. [52]

deficit The notion that some languages, some varieties of a language, or some individuals' language abilities are less complex and/or communicative than others. [14]

description The practice in linguistics of describing the varieties of a language without making value judgements about them or saying which variations are correct: cf. **prescription**. [15]

dialect Regional and social-class variety of a language which differs from the **standard** in pronunciation, grammar, and vocabulary. [13]

direct method Teaching an additional language without reference to or use of the students' first or other languages, in particular without translation. [33]

discourse analysis The study of how stretches of language in context are perceived as meaningful and unified by their users, and/or the study of how different uses of language constitute and express the values of social institutions. [50]

elaborated code A variety of a language said to have greater communicative resources than others. (A term first used by Basil Bernstein): cf. **restricted code**. [14]

ELF *See* **English as a Lingua Franca.**

ELT *See* **English Language Teaching.**

English as a Lingua Franca (ELF) A variety, or varieties, of English used as a means of communication between non-native speakers. *See also* **lingua franca**. [29]

English for Specific Purposes (ESP) English teaching which focuses upon the language and discourse skills needed for particular jobs (English for Occupational Purposes (EOP)) or for particular fields of study (English for Academic Purposes (EAP)). [37]

English Language Teaching (ELT) The teaching of English as a first or additional language. [30]

Englishes National varieties of English with their own rules and norms, e.g. Australian English, Indian English, Singapore English, American English. [27]

ESP *See* **English for Specific Purposes.**

expanding circle Countries where English is fast becoming a dominant second language in the domains of education, science, and technology, e.g. China, Japan, the countries of Europe. (A term first used by Braj Kachru.) [27]

feasibility Knowledge of whether and to what degree a given piece of language can be successfully processed, irrespective of whether it is a possible sequence. (The second parameter of Hymes' model of communicative competence.) [42]

first-language education Study of, and in, a child's home language or languages. [7]

foreign-language education Study of the language of another country which is not a necessary or official language in the student's own country. [7]

forensic linguistics The deployment of linguistic evidence in criminal and other legal investigations, e.g. to establish the authorship of a document, or a profile of a speaker from a tape-recording. [7]

functional linguistics The study of the forms of language with reference to their social function in communication. [9]

generative linguistics A programme of **linguistics**, initiated and developed by Noam Chomsky from the late 1950s onward, investigating language as a biologically endowed cognitive faculty. [9]

genre A type of discourse, either written or spoken, with particular conventional characteristics, e.g. conversation, email, opera. [52]

grammar-translation The teaching of an additional language through the learning of rules and vocabulary lists, and the written translation of graded invented sentences. [32]

information design The arrangement and presentation of written language, including issues relating to **typography** and layout, choices of medium, and effective combinations of language with other means of communication such as pictures and diagrams. [8]

inner circle The countries where English is the native language of the majority, e.g. Australia, Britain, Canada, New Zealand, and the USA. (A term first used by Braj Kachru.) [27]

interdisciplinarity The notion that the boundaries between traditional areas of enquiry should be dissolved in favour of enquiry which draws equally upon several areas. [78]

language death The complete disappearance of a language. [24]

language planning The making of decisions, often supported by legislation, about the official status of languages and their institutional use, including their use in education. [7]

language rights The rights of all people to have their language recognized and respected, taught to their children, and accepted in official communication. [57]

language testing The assessment and evaluation of language achievement and proficiency, in both additional and first languages, and for both general and specific purposes. [7]

lexicography The planning and compiling of both monolingual and bilingual dictionaries, and other language reference works such as thesauri. [8]

lingua franca A language used for communication between people speaking a variety of languages. Formerly, this term referred to a language which was not the first language of those involved. Now it often refers to any widely used language. *See also* **English as a Lingua Franca (ELF)**. [4, 57]

linguistic competence Knowledge of the grammar of a language as distinct from its actual use. [42]

linguistic relativity hypothesis The idea that a language partly or wholly determines the perception and categorization of reality. [59]

linguistics The academic discipline concerned with the study of language in general. [9]

literary stylistics The study of the relationship between linguistic choices and effects in literature. [8, 61]

machine translation The use of computer programs to provide a rough basis for how a given stretch of one language might be translated into another. [56]

mediation The way in which, in applied linguistics, theory makes reference to practice, and practice makes reference to theory. (A term first used by Henry Widdowson.) [10]

native speaker A notoriously difficult term to define, whose use is increasingly challenged. Traditionally, a person who, by virtue of having acquired a language in infancy and having continued to use it since, has a proficiency and intuition unattainable by others. [28]

natural approach Language 'teaching' without explanation, grading, or correction of errors, but only presentation of 'meaningful input'. [34]

needs analysis Identifying what learners will need to do with the language they are learning. [37]

nominalization The use of inanimate nouns to refer to actions and processes, thus omitting mention of who is responsible for them, e.g. 'Genetic modification is a powerful technique.' [66]

outer circle Countries, often former British colonies, where English is either an official language or widely used in administration and education, e.g. India, Nigeria, Singapore. (A term first used by Braj Kachru.) [27]

paralanguage Meaningful non-linguistic behaviour which accompanies linguistic communication, e.g. gestures and intonation in speech, or pictures and font choice in writing. [50]

passivization The favouring of passive constructions rather than active ones, with the effect of disguising who is responsible for an event, e.g. '*Redundancies will be announced.*' [66]

performance Chomsky's term for actual language behaviour as distinct from the knowledge that underlies it. [9]

possibility Knowledge of whether and to what degree a stretch of language conforms to the rules of its grammar. (The first parameter of Hymes' model of communicative competence.) [42]

pragmatics The study of the knowledge and procedures which enable people to understand each other's words. [51]

prescription An approach to a language claiming there are absolute fixed rules which should be followed by everyone: cf. **description**. [15]

psycholinguistics The study of language and the mind: the mental structures and processes which are involved in the acquisition and use of language. [37]

restricted code A variety of a language said to have fewer communicative resources than others. (A term first used by Basil Bernstein): cf. **elaborated code**. [14]

Second-Language Acquisition (SLA) How people acquire an additional language, often studied by means of an analysis of the errors they make. [31, 71]

second-language education The study of, or education in, the majority or official language of a student's society, which is not the student's main or home language. [7]

SLA *See* **Second-Language Acquisition**.

sociolinguistics The study of the relation between language and society: how social factors influence the structure and use of language. [9]

standard The variety of a language used in written communication, taught in schools, and codified in dictionaries and grammar books. [4, 13]

synthetic personality The way in which communication to people *en masse* appears to address them as individuals. (A term first used by Norman Fairclough.) [67]

Task-Based Instruction (TBI) An approach to language teaching in which learners must complete activities which aim to simulate real-world communicative problem solving, and in which attention is principally focused on meaning rather than form. [37]

TBI *See* **Task-Based Instruction**.

Teaching English as a Foreign Language (TEFL) The teaching of English to people of countries where it is not an official language. [26, 31]

TEFL *See* **Teaching English as a Foreign Language**.

translation and interpretation The formulation of principles underlying the perceived equivalence between a stretch of language and its translation, and the practices of translating written text and interpreting spoken language. [8]

translation studies The academic discipline concerned with the theory and practice of translation and interpreting. [55]

typography The study of the visual organization of written language however it is produced, e.g. by hand, printing press, or electronically, and of ways in which this organization can be used to aid understanding. [8]

Universal Grammar (UG) The grammatical properties shared by all human languages, claimed by Chomsky to be part of the genetic endowment of the human species. [42]

UG *See* **Universal Grammar.**

visual communication The use of visuals, such as pictures and diagrams, either alongside or instead of language, and the visual aspects of writing. [51]

workplace communication The study of how language is used in the workplace, and how it contributes to the nature and power relations in different types of work. [7]

Acknowledgements

The author and publisher are grateful to the following for permission to reproduce extracts from copyright material:

Arnold for extract from Rosamund Mitchell and Florence Myles: *Second Language Learning Theories* (Arnold 1998).

Blackwell Publishing for extract from Barbara Seidlhofer: 'Closing the conceptual gap: the case for a description of English as a lingua franca' in *International Journal of Applied Linguistics* Vol. 11/2, 2001.

Cambridge University Press for extract from Susan Hunston: *Corpora in Applied Linguistics* (The Cambridge Applied Linguistics Series 2002).

Carcanet Press Ltd. and New Directions Publishing Corporation for lines from William Carlos Williams: 'The Right of Way' from *Collected Poems: 1909–1939*, Vol. 1, copyright © 1938 by New Directions Publishing Corporation, used in extract from Robert Fowler: *Linguistic Criticism* (2nd edn., Oxford University Press 1996).

Georgetown University Press for extract from William Labov: 'The Logic of nonstandard English' first published in J. Alatis (ed.): *Georgetown Monographs on Language and Linguistics* Vol. 22, 1969.

Oxford University Press for extracts from Roger Fowler: *Linguistic Criticism* (2nd edn., Oxford University Press 1996); A. P. R. Howatt: *A History of Language Teaching* (Oxford University Press 1984), © A. P. R. Howatt 1984; Claire Kramsch: *Context and Culture in Language Teaching* (Oxford University Press 1993), © Claire Kramsch 1993; Robert Phillipson: *Linguistic Imperialism* (Oxford

University Press 1992), © R. H. L. Phillipson 1992; and Peter Skehan: *A Cognitive Approach to Language Learning* (Oxford University Press 1998), © Oxford University Press 1998; and for extracts from Michael Canale and Merrill Swain: 'Theoretical bases of communicative approaches to second language teaching and testing' in *Applied Linguistics* 1/1, 1980; and M. B. H. Rampton: 'Displacing the "native speaker": expertise, affiliation, and inheritance' in *ELT Journal* 44/2, 1990.

Sage Publishing Ltd for extract from Norman Fairclough and Ruth Wodak: 'Critical Discourse Analysis' in Teun A. van Dijk (ed.): *Discourse as Social Interaction*, Vol. 2 (Sage Publications 1997).

Taylor and Francis Books Ltd. for extracts from Mona Baker: *In Other Words: A coursebook on translation* (Routledge 1992), pp 4–5; Deborah Cameron: *Verbal Hygiene* (Routledge 1995), pp 3–4; and Malcolm Coulthard: 'The Official Version: Audience manipulation in police records of interviews with suspects' in C. R. Caldas-Coulthard and M. Coulthard (eds.): *Texts and Practices* (Routledge 1996), pp 166–167.

University of Pennsylvania Press for extract from Dell Hymes: 'On communicative competence' (University of Pennsylvania Press 1971), originally given at *Research Planning Conference on Language Development Among Disadvantaged Children*, Yeshiva University, June 1966.

Whurr Publishers Ltd for extracts from Michael Perkins and Sara Howard (eds.): *Case Studies in Clinical Linguistics* (Whurr Publishers 1995); from Michael Perkins and Sara Howard: 'Principles of clinical linguistics' pp 11–12, and from Julie Morris and Sue Franklin: 'Aphasia: assessment and remediation of a speech discrimination effect', pp 245–6.

Henry G. Widdowson for extracts from 'Models and Fictions' in H. G. Widdowson: *Explorations in Applied Linguistics* 2 (Oxford University Press 1984), and for extract from H. G. Widdowson: 'The ownership of English' in *TESOL Quarterly* 28/2, 1994.

Despite every effort to trace and contact copyright holders before publication, this has not been possible in every case. If notified, the publisher will be pleased to rectify any errors or omissions at the earliest opportunity.